# PRAISE FOR *WELL SENT*

"Steve Beirn is one of North America's most respected voices when it comes to being 'well sent.' I listen with keen interest every time Steve speaks, as he does so from much war-torn experience. As churches move from passive to active in the sending arena, we will need to learn from a number of pioneers who have blazed a trail ahead of us. Steve shares with conviction and heart in *Well Sent*, and I highly recommend it to those serious about the task of sending with excellence."

—Ron Burdock
Director of Global Outreach
North Park Community Church, Ontario

"This book is a beautiful demonstration of the maturing of the church in North America! Just as numerous areas of the world have matured in the realm of missions, so the church in the US has matured in important ways. This book, rooted in Scripture and seasoned by years of experience, provides an excellent guide for any local church, as part of the body of Christ, to actively and effectively send laborers into the harvest."

—Dr. Stephen Coffey
US Director of Christar

"Steve has written a book that many of us in local churches have longed for. From a practitioner who understands the times, *Well Sent* is a compassionate, yet straightforward, treatise that places the focus of sending global workers right where it needs to be—the local church. Through biblical insights, mission realities and Steve's personal experience, this book presents not just a 'wake up call,' but practical lessons to incorporate into the missions DNA of your church. Read it, learn from it, apply it, teach others from it—and you will see a fresh and exciting commitment to God's global mission within your church."

—Bruce Huseby
Pastor of Global Ministries
Calvary Church, Grand Rapids


"*Well Sent* is a reliable, biblical and practical guide to developing a missions-minded church. The appendices alone are worth the effort to 'reimage the church's missionary sending process.' I heartily endorse this book for helping build a God-honoring, missions-minded church."

—Robertson McQuilkin
President Emeritus of Columbia International University

"When it comes to understanding the inner workings of sending and supporting missionaries, Steve brings experience, knowledge and biblical insight to the conversation. As one who owns the responsibility to fulfill the Great Commission, he provides us with a thoughtful examination of the church's role in global engagement. But, thankfully, this work is not merely a theoretical treatise. Steve's book is written to address the real-world challenges a sending church will face. I will be recommending *Well Sent* as a practical resource to guide mission-minded leaders through the sending process."

—Kevin Oessenich
Executive Director of World Team USA

"I recommend *Well Sent: Reimagining the Church's Missionary-Sending Process* because it is both encyclopedic in scope and cookbook in style and usefulness. The book includes more than sufficient analysis and creative thinking to engage the best minds in churches and mission agencies. Plus, it is very practical because Beirn and Murray spice up their ideas with stories from their long and distinguished careers as missions pastor (Beirn) and agency executive (Murray). Their exquisite balance between theory and practice makes *Well Sent* a truly valuable resource, which, if applied, could greatly strengthen what appears to be a serious weakness in how we recruit and send missionaries."

—Jim Reapsome
Editor of *Evangelical Missions Quarterly*, 1964-97

"Churches don't get excited about missions until they send their own people. Step-by-step, *Well Sent* will walk you through how to train and send your own people. This book is a must-read for local church missions leadership."

—Tom Telford
Missions Mobilizer with United World Mission

"In *Well Sent*, Steve Beirn wades into an important and hotly debated question and gives us insights from and for the 'real world,' regarding the role of North America and global missions today. Beirn provides a biblically rooted and personally engaged take on the *missio Dei* for today. Steve is a realist calling the church to obey and go, wherever and whenever, while being mindful of the era it lives in as it pursues its timeless commission."

—Scott White
Associate Pastor of Missions and Evangelism
Pastor of Global Outreach
Lake Avenue Church

# WELL SENT

# WELL SENT

## REIMAGINING THE CHURCH'S MISSIONARY-SENDING PROCESS

### STEVE BEIRN
#### WITH
#### GEORGE W. MURRAY

**CLC**
**PUBLICATIONS**
Fort Washington, PA 19034

*Well Sent*
Published by CLC Publications

*USA:* P.O. Box 1449, Fort Washington, PA 19034
www.clcpublications.com

*UK:* Kingsway CLC Trust
Unit 5, Glendale Avenue, Sandycroft, Flintshire, CH5 2QP
www.equippingthechurch.com

This printing 2023

Printed in the United States of America


ISBN (paperback): 978-1-61958-211-8
ISBN (e-book): 978-1-61958-212-5

Italics in Scripture quotations are the emphasis of the author.

# CONTENTS

FOREWORD   11

ACKNOWLEDGEMENTS   15

INTRODUCTION   17

PART 1: OWNING THE CHURCH'S SPECIAL TASK

  1   The Perception of Sending: Why Has Sending Lost Its Way?   27

  2   The Basis for Sending: How Does the Bible Endorse It?   45

  3   The Blessing of Sending: How Is It Personal and Energizing?   59

PART 2: OWNING THE CHURCH'S SPECIAL PATH

  4   The Mobilization Keys: What Can Fortify the Church?   73

  5   The Mobilization Role: How Does the Church Contribute?   87

  6   The Evaluation Role: How and Why Does the Church
      Evaluate a Missionary Call?   97

PART 3: OWNING THE CHURCH'S SPECIAL RELATIONSHIPS

  7   The Functional Relationship   109

  8   The Strategic Relationship: What Are the Remaining Unfinished Tasks?   123

PART 4: OWNING THE CHURCH'S SPECIAL CHALLENGES

  9   The Danger in Becoming a Sending-Church Model   139

 10   The Danger of Distractions: What Keeps the Church from
      Being Effective Senders?   151

 11   Identifying a Sending Church   163

# APPENDIXES

Appendix 1   Building a Robust Faith for You or Your Church                    175

Appendix 2   PAC Team Brochure                                                 177

Appendix 3   Global Partner Candidate Bimonthly Worksheet                      181

Appendix 4   Global Ministries Prayer Initiative for 2014–2016                 185

Appendix 5   The Church/Agency/Missionary Sending-Triangle Worksheet           187

Appendix 6   Categorizing Your Church                                          193

Appendix 7   Release of Information                                            195

Appendix 8   Measuring Agency Partnership Potential                            199

Appendix 9   Global Ministries Position Paper                                  209

Appendix 10   Know Your Church Audience                                        215

NOTES                                                                          221

# FOREWORD

A s the drama of the book of Acts plays out across the New Testament stage, one local church is given a pivotal role. Antioch in those days was an outpost on the fringes of the Christian world. Five of its leaders had come together to worship and fast. Suddenly, God motions them from the wings to center stage. Acts 13 records that He directs them to set apart two of their team for key roles—missionary roles—in His unfolding drama of church expansion.

Why wasn't the Jerusalem Council in the spotlight for this task of missionary sending? Or couldn't the Holy Spirit simply have handed Paul and Barnabas their parts directly? Instead, God very intentionally chose to give local church leaders a pivotal role in launching the first New Testament missionary team.

Sadly, since that time the majority of local churches have retreated to the wings, content to play only supporting roles in this most important drama. Yes, many congregations have loved missionaries, and given to and prayed for them. But incredibly, generations of faithful pastors have preached through the book of Acts but failed to see themselves in the Acts 13 role of missionary selectors and senders. Instead they delegated this key task to others.

That is, until recently. Calvary Church of Lancaster, Pennsylvania is one of a growing number of contemporary congregations that is embracing their biblical role in discerning the Spirit's selection of global workers from their midst, and then proactively sending them into the harvest.

I believe Acts 13 illustrates that no missionary is well sent without the prayerful, proactive sending of their local body. However, the "how" of that sending process is left up to the church. In *Well Sent*, Missions Pastor Steve Beirn lays the foundational principles for biblical sending and shares many practical how-tos for fulfilling the church's mobilization role. While Calvary is a large church, the strategy Steve shares here is not dependent on professional staff or a large budget. Regardless of your congregation's size or experience, you will find a wealth of ideas to implement.

But sending well takes work! It is a ministry-long process that demands the church, the missionary and the agency collaborate consistently. Good sending starts years before the missionary's appointment. And if the worker has extended service, it may involve passing the "sending baton" from one generation of church leaders to the next. This manual has been written to help local churches establish and sustain their fulfillment of that strategic sending role.

"I wish I had a sending church like that!" I've heard many missionaries wistfully say as they saw how another worker's local church practiced sending. Your congregation can be one of those starring churches!

In these pages, Steve unpacks proven guidelines for becoming a successful sending congregation in the Antioch tradition.

God's drama is still playing out across the global stage today. More Pauls and Barnabases are waiting in the wings for their church to commission and deploy them for key roles in the ongoing story of world missions. Church, you've been called into the spotlight of God's global drama to be senders. Don't miss your cue. This book will help you play your role well!

Ellen Livingood
President, Catalyst Services

# ACKNOWLEDGEMENTS

I t goes without saying that any book project is a group project. There are numerous people to thank. My deepest appreciation goes to my wife, Lorraine. She has encouraged and prayed for me throughout this process. Her effort on the laptop and time spent discussing content was remarkable. She has been the consummate life partner in both my personal and professional life. She is a gift from God.

I also want to thank George Murray, who agreed to work on the book with me. Although this represented quite a workload, he unselfishly gave time to contribute. Our many years of friendship have deepened through this project.

It is important to thank Dave Almack who serves as the National Director of CLC USA. Dave believed there was a potential book in my ministry emphasis. He pursued both me and this book in gracious and affirming ways. His staff was of wonderful assistance. My thanks to Erika Cobb, Laura Pollard and Scott Endicott for their guidance and unique help in developing and providing a finished project.

To the leadership of Calvary Church, I am deeply grateful. The brief sabbatical provided a block of time to really move the project forward. I felt like I had a team of encouragers throughout the writing process.

Finally, I want to thank Ellen Livingood. She has spoken into a variety of concepts found in the book. Her ability to help me refine my thoughts has been so needed. She has also provided several resources in the appendix that will prove valuable for churches. Catalyst Services and Calvary Church share a passion to equip and serve other churches. We both trust and pray that many will be helped as a result of our group effort.

# INTRODUCTION

Sending out missionaries has fallen on hard times. Traditionally strong sending countries are finding it increasingly difficult to meet the need for cross-cultural workers. Some postcolonial theology has valued indigenous culture and leaders to the point of becoming antimissionary. With the emergence of partnerships, the international justice movement, compassion ministries and supporting nationals, sending is more frequently perceived as an outdated ministry paradigm. The perception of sending and the urgency to send has changed over the last twenty to thirty years. This has impacted the ability of churches to accelerate the completion of the Great Commission.

This book seeks to elevate the role of the local church in the sending effort. The trend in missions today is to place the individual at the center of the sending process. Sometimes the agency is placed at the center. This book places the local church at the center of the sending process. Positioning the church at the center is not only biblically sound, it accomplishes what the individual or agency cannot easily do. It increases the flow of the workers and resources needed to accomplish the task. While other approaches can contribute, they also have greater limitations. Further, the church in general does not know what effective twenty-first-century sending practices look like. I believe we can identify these practices and equip the church to more effectively fulfill her commission. This book will describe what a vibrant sending commitment can look like in a local church that sends with precision.

I have often asked mission agencies if they were involved in equipping churches to send missionaries. Most agencies were not in any way involved in a significant equipping effort. This challenged me to develop material to assist the local church in the sending process. Out of this material, I developed a one-day conference called Ignite. Then I was asked by agency leaders and local church missions leaders to develop a book from this material.

Over the years, the local church has struggled to effectively assert itself in making disciples among all nations. There have been external struggles. Political, economic and technological changes can paralyze the church. Some internal struggles have impacted its ability to engage the world. Misplaced priorities, a lack of leadership and apathy have weakened the church. There are so many issues for the church to consider that people are overwhelmed. Often the result is that people don't know where to begin helping their church.

There is a need for the average missions practitioner to be better equipped to move the church forward. First, the local church needs to reassume more ownership of the missionary-sending process. Once the church understands and embraces its strategic role in sending, it will be able to address these and other issues that naturally follow.

A second reason this book was written was to provide healthy ways the church and mission agency can work together. The local church is largely dependent on dedicated volunteers to shape, manage, promote and advance missions. As the church goes, however, so goes the mission agency. More understanding will bring better working relationships. Hopefully this book will help local churches and mission agencies identify talking points and develop true partnerships.

A conservative estimate on the number of churches per "preferred" mission agency is twelve thousand to twelve. Are these agencies getting even one recruit from each church in spite of years of effort with these churches? These churches already have some relationship with world missions and desire to be relevant participants, but their lack of knowledge regarding their potential role as senders cripples them. Plus, the cacophony of voices crying out for attention has caused many missions programs to become stagnant, die or fade into irrelevance. The churches are growing, but their missions influence is waning—even though they previously had a strong missions tradition.

In addition to a diminished perspective on sending, the local church has not remained at the center of sending. Often, the individual considering global ministry is at the center of the process, partly due to the fact that the church has not assumed ownership. Agencies, by default and because of their expertise in global ministry, become front and center in the process. How can local churches once again assume ownership over the sending process while developing meaningful relationships with the individual and the agency? Are there compelling reasons why they should? This book will explain why and how this should take place and will present a pathway for the local church to build or strengthen its shepherding process for sending out candidates cross-culturally. Prepared churches can increase both the flow of workers and the flow of resources to accomplish the unfinished task. This process will not only fortify the church to effectively mobilize and send, but will also energize the church with new meaning and focus.

Within a growing number of churches, there is a faithful group of people whom God is using to advance the cause of reaching all nations for Christ. These people are, at their own expense, buying books and attending conferences to learn how to be involved globally and how to ignite this passion within their church. Agency leaders and representatives face exploding populations of unreached peoples, yet many of their missionaries are beginning to retire. Millennial young adults are interested in making their lives count but are unsure of the steps to take. All of these groups have something in common: they have lost sight of the example given us in the Word of God that the church is to be prepared to be the center of the sending process.

This book can be the key to unlock the potential for more global partners—the ones who are presently sitting in the pews. This book will describe what a vibrant sending commitment should look like in a local church that sends with precision. The individual seeking to follow Christ's command to make disciples of all nations will learn how vital it is to commit to and be sent out by a local church. That local church will be better equipped to guide and support that individual, and mission agencies will be able to support the local church leadership by casting vision and providing additional global ministry expertise.

A third purpose of this book is to better educate individuals who may be on the periphery of the local church and its vital role in sending. There is a generation of young adults who may have a connection to a discipling organization, or who may have visited various churches, but have never been encouraged to commit to a local church. Many think all they need is a desire to go, an agency to facilitate and people to contribute money. Hopefully, this book can help those who are interested in missions see the importance of developing a meaningful relationship and partnership with a local church. In addition to financial support, such partnerships allow church leadership and mentors to encourage and guide potential missionaries and to advance the vision of reaching and discipling all nations with the gospel of Jesus Christ.

This book is divided into four main sections. Each section will focus on vital elements of sending. Additionally, suggestions are made on how a church can assume ownership of these tasks. At the end of most of the chapters are action points, which are designed to help the reader bridge the concepts into their own life or church. These action points may be the most important part of the book as they will help readers apply the information learned. They can greatly contribute to strengthening any church's missions efforts. This book is meant to be accessible not only to the missions practitioner but also to the church volunteer, missions committee member or potential missionary candidate. I recommend that missions leadership teams read and discuss this book together.

I am grateful for the valuable contributions to this book from Dr. George Murray, chancellor of Columbia International University (CIU) in Columbia, South Carolina. He has graciously contributed the chapter "The Basis for Sending," as well as portions of "The Strategic Relationship" and "The Danger of Distractions." He brings expertise and perspective—having been a missionary, the general director for the mission agency Bible Christian Union (BCU) and the executive director of The Evangelical Alliance Mission (TEAM). He is a gifted speaker, teacher, writer and motivator whom God has used to challenge the church with the unfinished task.

In the appendix there are resources, examples and documents that can help local churches develop, reorganize or revitalize their missions programs. These are the result of years of practical implementation within the local church and have been prepared and included for the many unnoticed, seldom-recognized individuals who unselfishly give their time to missions.

Allow this book to provoke discussion and ideas. We have a deep love for the local church and the sending process, and we trust that this book will be an encouragement and a call to action as well as the spark to re-ignite the local church's flames of passion to reach the as-yet unreached.

# PART 1

OWNING THE CHURCH'S SPECIAL TASK

# 1

# THE PERCEPTION OF SENDING
## WHY HAS SENDING LOST ITS WAY?

Many believers today are guilty of rushing to judge missionary sending. Most have never seen a healthy church model in action. It is time for us to examine common misconceptions about sending and offer a more accurate assessment of this ministry model for the local church. Stepping into this forward-looking role will require a robust faith. Our personal ownership of the Great Commission mandate does not end where another person's begins. We are to own it together. There is no expiration date on a church or individual fully embracing the Great Commission.

On one occasion, I was in the Chicago area for a mission-agency board meeting. A small group of mission-agency personnel, along with a few local church people, were relaxing together over dinner. Everyone had just finished a full day of ministry responsibilities. After some entertaining discussion, the conversation changed. It turned to the dwindling numbers of new missionary recruits. With concern in their voices, several shared that the quality and quantity of potential missionaries was decreasing. Then I asked the question: How many agencies are equipping the local church to recruit their own missionaries? After a long pause, one person admitted that he'd never thought of approaching recruiting that way before. Others acknowledged that they weren't sure what it would look like to equip churches. No one had ever searched for any local church ministry models that pursued this approach. What would this type of ministry model offer the mission agency? At the end of a stimulating discussion, I volunteered to put together a document. It would describe what this ministry model would offer others in the missions world. It would explain how churches could be equipped to recruit future missionaries. It would be an attempt to have the local church share ownership of missionary sending. It could potentially assist the church in becoming a leader in missionary sending. This is what started the process that resulted in this book.

> "The exciting thing is that God
> is not done writing this story."

Think about this: Why, with the needs of the world visible via computers, smart phones and TVs, are we seeing such a limited response in our churches to the call to make disciples of all nations? It is easy to learn about the most remote locations of the world. Transportation makes it possible to get anywhere on the globe within twenty-four hours. Technology allows missionaries to stay fairly connected to their family and friends. Yet, agencies and churches seldom realize their full sending potential. This may be related to the way missions work is valued and workers are recruited. How can a church become a strategic partner in sending people out to the ends of the earth? What can an individual do to connect with a church that is willing and capable to send them out with the skills and prayer support they need? We need to start addressing these questions in order to equip the local-church to move from the sidelines into the game.

---

## "We are to own it together."

---

I am the Global Ministries pastor of a large sending church. In the seventy-seven years of our church history, we have sent more than four hundred of our own members overseas in cross-cultural ministry. This averages more than five workers for every year we have existed. An important part of our history is that missions has never been seen as a piece of the ministry pie but as the hub of a wheel, central to everything. Presently, we have 111 members serving around the globe. The price tag for all of this is breathtaking. Since we sent out our first missionary, prior to World War II, our sending has grown, despite many other conflicts and world crises. Our Global Ministries budget is 2.5 million dollars per year. It has been a wonderful story that God has authored. He alone is recognized as the architect of anything worthwhile. The exciting thing is that God is not done writing this story. This is an experienced ministry that has faced many challenges and learned many lessons in the journey to sustain faithful obedience to the Great Commission.

Many people are aware of the significant amount of missionary-sending activity that took place immediately following World War II. Churches embraced their returning soldiers and heard one stirring account after another of their many life experiences. These servicemen and women were deeply moved by the appalling spiritual needs of the world. As a result, other individuals shared their burdened heart for the world. Churches responded by sending out record numbers of new missionaries. Former military were even responsible for establishing new mission organizations. Robert Evans, in his book *Let Europe Hear*, points out that several hundred new missionaries left for Europe after the war. More than a dozen mission agencies and service groups were also created. East Asia saw a similar movement of missionaries. All this was done for the purpose of building the church in the former European and Asian theaters of war.[1]

This was surely a high point in missions. But, in my opinion, this strong sending emphasis began to dissipate by 1980. Though many new missionaries continued to go, churches began to simply maintain a borrowed momentum from the previous generation. The numbers of older missionaries became noticeable. Gradually, the sending process began to be perceived as the contribution of previous generations. Sending felt dated.

How did the church respond to this perception? Newer approaches to cross-cultural ministry emerged and were embraced by younger generations. In North America, we saw the beginnings of short-term work, support of nationals and the extensive use of radio. By the turn of the century, the church had embraced partnerships, relief and development, technology and social justice. These ministry efforts have received more time and attention from the church.

> "There is no expiration date on a church or individual fully embracing the Great Commission."

While God is certainly using a wide variety of these ministries to get His work done, there has been a noticeable diminishing of sending capacity within many churches. The end result is that sending is, in many circles, increasingly seen as antiquated or simply optional. David Horner, in his book *When Missions Shapes the Mission,* shares about his Southern Baptist denomination, which is often seen as a leader among evangelicals. With almost forty-five thousand churches affiliated with the denomination, the International Mission Board (IMB) has 5,656 full-time missionaries currently overseas. Many of the couples come from the same church, with a number of churches sustaining multiple families. This means that over 80 percent of all these churches have not sent anyone overseas. The denomination points out, "Nearly 90 percent of the models to which pastors are exposed have not demonstrated a functional commitment to missions. In the absence of such models, what else would pastors assume but that their ministry is normal if they only occasionally tip their hat to the mandate Christ has given for missions."[2]

---

"There has been a noticeable diminishing of sending capacity within many churches."

---

All generations want to own their own ministry commitments. Sometimes these ministry commitments take the church into unknown, yet productive, territory. Other times, they pull the church away from its focus of making disciples of all the nations. Unfortunately, perception is often reality with missionary sending. The good news, however, is that there are a number of young churches today that heavily stress sending out their own people as missionaries overseas. I am once again seeing traction with sending-church models. Every year, three to five (big and small) churches contact me looking for help to start or rekindle sending. So the first issue affecting missionary sending is the perception that it is an antiquated system.

A second issue that has influenced our attitude toward sending is postcolonial theology. This theology has valued indigenous culture and leaders to a point of becoming antimissionary. Western missionaries sent out over the last one hundred years have made mistakes.

There are reasons why some antimissionary and anti-Western sentiments exist. No one wants to minimize these painful memories. An honest evaluation should inform everyone about improving ministry practices rather than abandoning ministry efforts.

In the January/February 2014 issue of *Christianity Today*, Andrea Palpant Dilley wrote a significant article entitled "The World the Missionaries Made." The article describes the scholarly research, considered sophisticated and well-grounded, of Dr. Robert Woodberry. Dr. Woodberry is quoted as saying, "One stereotype about missions is that they were closely connected to colonialism. But Protestant missionaries not funded by the state were regularly very critical of colonialism."[3] William Carey, "the Father of Modern Missions," preached about five basic principles of ministry. Principle four was: "Missionaries should carry on a profound study of the culture and thought of the people among whom they were to minister."[4] In 1890, Dr. John Nevius, a missionary in China, visited Korea and shared his four indispensable missionary principles. His second principle is: "Church methods and organizational structures should only be developed as far as the Korean church can take responsibility for them."[5] Dr. Donald McGavran much later on emphasized, "Evangelism should be culturally sensitive."[6] An unfortunate side to missions history exists, and we can benefit from acknowledging and learning from this history. The errors of the past do not negate the command to continue to cross barriers of distance, language and culture to deliver the good news.

Economics have also played into the antimissionary mind-set. Robertson McQuilkin tells of a full-page ad that appeared in *Christianity Today* and said, "Thank you for not coming." It was a promotional effort to get North American money—not missionaries. McQuilkin writes, "'Let the nationals do it.' They have the language and culture and, most important, they cost so much less. True enough, but what about the dark one-third of the world where there are no 'nationals,' no witnessing church?"[7]

There is another issue that may cause us to concentrate on our local responsibilities to the exclusion of the rest of the world. There are some who believe that Acts 1:8 is to be interpreted sequentially. They believe that Jerusalem is their first priority and that Judea, Samaria and the ends of the earth move up the list as each preceding focus is fully engaged. Marvin Newell, in his book *Commissioned,* states that the spreading of the gospel was never intended to be a three-step process, nor was there any intention to establish a center for all ministry activity. The language in the text supports a simultaneous witness. The text says, "Jerusalem and in all Judea and Samaria, and to the end of the earth." Newell points out,

> "The nature of the global mission of the church demands that it should never establish one geographical center. Jesus wanting to make sure the disciples did not establish Jerusalem as its center, explicitly told them to go out from the city. The Old Testament version of centripetal mission, where Israel welcomed all nations streaming to it was to be replaced by the centrifugal mission of going out to the nations. Christianity was not to be an ethnically

Jewish-centric religion, a linguistically Hebrew-centric religion or a geographically Jerusalem-centric religion."[8]

The implication therefore is to engage the world. Each church should consider how it can develop a simultaneous witness here, nearby and around the world that could utilize sending as a result.

In spite of the obvious needs of the unreached, there is a natural pull for a church to have a "Jerusalem first" approach to ministry. Paul Borthwick points out, "Some churches, overwhelmed and 'globophobic,' choose to do little or nothing. Small budgets, survival mentalities and local challenges predominate. The do little/do nothing perspective was summed up by one pastor serving in a community struggling with an unemployment rate exceeding 22 percent. He told me, 'I can scarcely do enough to serve the needs in my own congregation and you want me to think about *the world*?'" Borthwick continues to share his initial thought about a similar mentality in North America. He states, "When North American Christians tell me that they or their church is not concerned about or involved in the Majority World church because 'the needs are so great here at home,' I wonder if the issue is actually local need. Sometimes I wonder whether this phrase represents a protective desire to shield ourselves from sacrificial challenges."[9] In my interaction with churches I have found this to be more than a hunch.

First of all, the needs here in North America pale in comparison to needs overseas. The likelihood that people overseas have an equal opportunity to hear an understandable presentation of the gospel as in North America is extremely small. In some areas of the world they have no opportunity to hear—even if they want to hear. Dr. Robertson McQuilkin had a family member who served as a missionary in Calcutta, India and reflected on the comparison with Columbia, South Carolina.

> "In America, one out of five people you do business with or meet at the PTA will be a Bible-believing Christian; in Calcutta, one out of ten thousand. And how many Bibles are in Columbia, South Carolina? A million? Calcutta may have a few hundred and for many of the languages in that great city, none at all. In a population of three hundred thousand, we have at least six hundred churches. In that city, among the five million slum dwellers, there are perhaps five small fellowships. We have three or four Christian radio stations, they none, we have at least fifteen Christian bookstores, they none. No wonder we have perhaps a hundred thousand evangelical believers and they about one thousand."[10]

Todd Ahrend, in his book *In This Generation*, provides an additional perspective on assessing spiritual need. He shares this experience:

> "I couldn't have gotten two more opposite phone calls in one day—if they had been separated by a week maybe, but one day? The first was a friend of mine who called to inform me that a missions trip his agency was planning had just been canceled. They could not find a team of five to go to North Africa on a short-term mission trip. Zero applicants. Two hours later my pastor friend called me. He sounded

really stressed so I asked him what was going on. He said he had put out an ad to hire a youth pastor and had received over sixty applicants in two weeks. He could not even look through them all. He was drowning in responses."[11]

Some believe that you are practicing hypocrisy when you focus on overseas ministry rather than local opportunities. When you understand the nature of the good news, you realize that an either/or approach to local/global is an inadequate response. This mind-set draws people away from the challenge of a balanced, simultaneous approach to ministry. Follow the simple pattern of pray, give, serve and witness. Some of these options place no limits on your involvement, while others do. Select what is appropriate for your Jerusalem, Judea, Samaria and the ends of the earth.

Churches can be overwhelmed by the enormity of the task; others simply are paralyzed by fear when they think about entering this unpredictable world. Experiencing these reactions is one thing. Living with these visceral reactions is quite another matter. No one likes the idea that his or her life is out of control and unpredictable. Yet, we have an all-sufficient God who is in control. We need to learn to live in the light of this truth. We need to realize that every day is a theology test. Eric Wright, in his book *A Practical Theology of Missions,* has a chapter entitled "Absentee Landlord or Reigning King?" This captures the real issue. The answer to many natural concerns or fears is the building of a robust faith, either as a church or as an individual.

Unfortunately, many have not yet taken this journey. Michael Ramsden says, "Our goal is not to conserve our lives at any cost but rather to live our life in obedience to the call we have received. We are not called to ignore risk or to be reckless. Everything must be prayerfully considered."[12] It is easy to build our lives around comfort, security and convenience, and so we do. The Scriptures have a different emphasis. We are afraid that a life of faith, stepping up to the challenge of leaving the familiar for the unknown, must naturally be miserable and severe. I have often said that you don't have to have an easy life in order to have a joyful life. Just look at Acts 16 and the life of Paul and Silas while on a missionary journey. Building a robust faith will change you and many others where you live and potentially around the world (Appendix 1). If we do not build a robust faith, the North American church may lose its institutional will to respond to hardship and opposition.

> "Nothing moves outside and independent
> of God's sovereign plans."

In my church-ministry experience, we have had several deep challenges to our faith. In 1981, we experienced the kidnapping and martyrdom of one of our missionaries. An experience like that causes you to more carefully count the cost. The parents of our martyred missionary wrote me a note that simply said, "In appreciation for your prayer and expressions of love to us during this special time in our lives." I still have that note. In some mysterious way, God's grace proved sufficient. Beyond the trauma of that experience, many revisited their convictions and moved forward in their obedience to the Great Commission. The two fundamental convictions that continue to propel us all forward are the sovereignty of God and the necessity of the gospel. Nothing moves outside and independent of God's sovereign plans.[13] There will always be circumstances that are difficult or impossible for us to interpret. Yet this is a part of our walk of faith. We also know that God uses suffering for our good and the spread of the gospel. It is equally true that salvation is based on specific, receptive trust in Jesus Christ alone.[14] Why is this so important? It establishes Jesus Christ as the only answer for all mankind. When you think about this truth, it can take your breath away. We must develop some settled convictions in order to take the gospel forward in our unpredictable world. Mark Morris is the director for the Advancement of Nontraditional Church Strategies for the International Mission Board. Recently, he wrote an article entitled, "A Theology of Strategic Risk in the Advancement of the Gospel." He states, "As an individual, church leader, member of a congregation or a representative of a mission agency, we should not assume that God gives us permission to prioritize safety and security over and above the advancement of God's mission and the preaching of His gospel."[15] Our fears and apprehensions should be extinguished over time by a flood of eternal truth.

Another issue that has impacted the way we think and engage in sending missionaries is the rise of the global south. Over the last two or three decades, we have seen the explosive expansion of church growth in the southern hemisphere. The center of Christian influence and activity continues to move south. In his book *Pressure Points*, J.D. Payne states, "Today the largest number of Christ followers live outside of the western world."[16] If the numerical growth of the church continues at its present pace, by 2025 the largest Christian communities may be Brazil, the Philippines, Nigeria, the Democratic Republic of the Congo and South India. This growth has resulted in many believers going into all the world to share the gospel. We all know about the "back to Jerusalem" movement that was birthed out of the house church movement in China. These churches are calling for one hundred thousand new missionaries to be sent out across Asia and back to Jerusalem. Over twenty thousand South Korean missionaries are scattered around the globe. One of the largest mission agencies in the world presently is in Brazil. The church in the Philippines, India, Nigeria and Indonesia is sending out a volume of new workers cross-culturally. Several years ago, I participated in a missions conference at the Central American Theological Seminary in Guatemala City. It was a gathering of key missions leaders. The conference drew church leaders from almost every Latin American country. I was invited to conduct several workshops on how the global north and south can work together to build the church. I came away with two very strong impressions. The first was the level of energy and vision that the Latin church possesses for the world. I was incredibly blessed and encouraged by this. The second impression was how much we both need each other. Our different life experiences, resources and skill sets need to be brought together to accelerate the growth of the church. In the middle of all this encouraging global growth, it would be tragic to assume that the North American church need not send any more missionaries.

> "Building your robust faith will change you and many others where you live and potentially around the world."

Some have used the image of a relay race to describe the North American church passing the baton to the Latin, Korean or African church. Paul Borthwick states: "The image helpfully depicts some good changes and the change to majority world leadership. The image breaks down, however, in this regard: when the leader passes the baton to the next runner, the former leader stops running. Truly implementing this image would mean that the North American church needs to drop out of the race."[17] Considering the growth of the majority world church, J.D. Payne draws this conclusion: "The truth is that the Great Commission of Jesus is just as binding on Western churches as it is on Majority World churches. For those of us in the West to abdicate our missionary labors among the nations is a direct violation of the call of Christ on our lives."[18] There are still so many people groups that have yet to hear the gospel. North Americans should not make an assumption that all the remaining work can or should be done by the majority world. Our personal ownership of the Great Commission mandate does not end where another person's begins. We are to own it together. There is no expiration date on a church or individual fully embracing the Great Commission.

"God uses suffering for our good to spread of the gospel."

One final issue that has impacted the sending-church effort is the rise of compassion ministries. Over the years, the term "holistic" has been used to describe ministry that has an emphasis on the body and the soul. It is a ministry approach that delivers the gospel in word and deed. This has been an effective ministry approach over the years. It has been desperately needed in certain ministry contexts due to the level of physical suffering present. Some audiences might become nervous about holistic ministry as there have been occasions when the gospel was only shared in deed. It has at times been disappointing to find a so-called holistic ministry built entirely on good works. In this type of ministry effort there is simply no recognition of time and eternity. "Eternal thinking is realizing that our circumstances matter to God, but they matter in the context of eternity."[19] We need to understand that poverty may be all around us or even inside us. The interest in holistic ministry has continued to resonate with many in the church. The emergence of social justice and other compassion ministries within the last ten to fifteen years has fostered a new conscience within the local church around the world.

I have personally seen the terrible consequences of human trafficking in Cambodia. Women have shared their survival stories with me, and I have been deeply moved. When I was shown a brothel that had recently been shut down, I registered a response somewhere between heartbreak and horror. Addressing human suffering has at times resembled the fervor of a crusade. People have seen this cause as an ideal way to channel their time and energy. It has provided people with an opportunity to make a difference. It has captured the imagination of many younger adults within the church. However, this new allure has at times overshadowed the mandate of the church. My appeal would be to develop a fervor for both compassion ministries and the mandate. In *What Is the Mission of the Church?*, authors Kevin DeYoung and Greg Gilbert say, "Don't undersell what the Bible says about the poor and social justice."[20] The Scriptures give serious time and attention to justice and the poor.

The balance in all this is to equally embrace the unique task of the church. DeYoung and Gilbert continue, "We want the crystal-clear and utterly unique task of the church—making disciples of Jesus Christ to the glory of God the Father—put front and center, not lost in a flurry of commendable concerns."[21] They also write, "This mission is a specific set of things Jesus has sent his church into the world to accomplish and is significantly narrower than 'everything God commands.'"[22] There have been numerous occasions on which social justice and the missionary mandate have overlapped to honor

God. Missions history is full of examples of social justice pursued by the church and missionaries. The need is still great for missionaries to be sent out to address both physical and spiritual poverty.

# 2

# THE BASIS FOR SENDING

## HOW DOES THE BIBLE ENDORSE IT?

### by George W. Murray

Every individual and church needs to reflect on the question: Is missionary sending an issue of methodology, or is sending a biblical practice? This chapter will explain that missionaries don't just *go* to the lost; they are *sent* to the lost. The local church is responsible to release and send workers to those still waiting for the good news. Missions is God's work of bringing Jesus Christ to a world who needs Him, through you.

Is the sending out of missionaries by local churches biblical? Is this something that God's Word teaches, or is it just something that we have traditionally done? A close look at Scripture reveals that God's missionary-sending heart is pervasive throughout the Bible, in both the Old and New Testaments. Any careful reader of the Bible will discover that missionary sending is not just something we might do—it is something we must do. Missionary sending is not just an option—it is an obligation.

Dr. Henrietta Mears, author of *What the Bible Is All About*, is known to frequently say, "The Bible does not talk about hundreds of different things; the Bible talks about one thing in hundreds of different ways." That is a profound and accurate statement. The one thing the Bible talks about is best described with two words: redemption and missions. When people hear me say this, they often exclaim, "Oh, you say that because you and your wife were missionaries!" And I reply, "No, my wife and I were missionaries because redemption and missions are the one thing the Bible is talking about!"

Let's look at and define these two terms that describe the one thing that the Bible is talking about. What is redemption? Redemption is God's work of bringing Jesus Christ to a world who needs Him. Ever since the fall of mankind into sin and even before that, in His eternal counsels, a just and gracious God has been working to bring Jesus Christ to the world. In fact, in Revelation 13:8 Jesus Christ is called "the Lamb slain from the foundation of the world" (KJV). God clearly alluded to this when He said to the serpent, Satan, right after Adam and Eve's disobedience, "He [the offspring of the woman, Jesus Christ] shall bruise your head, and you shall bruise his heel" (Gen. 3:15). The entire sacrificial system, instituted by God in the early pages of the Old Testament, was designed to point to the ultimate sacrifice of Jesus Christ, who was announced by John the Baptist to be "the Lamb of God, who takes away the sin of the world!" (John 1:29).

What is missions? Missions is God's work of bringing Jesus Christ to a world that needs Him, enacted through His people. This is the story of the Old Testament. This is the story of the New Testament. This is the one thing that the Bible is talking about. The mission field is "the world" (anywhere where people are), and the missionary is "you" (anyone who is committed to the Lord). That means a person is either a missionary (knows the Lord as his or her personal Savior) or a mission field (does not know the Lord as his or her personal Savior). This is true in the general sense; but later on in this book, we will show that in the technical sense, not all true Christians are "missionaries," nor should they be, and not all areas or people groups in the world can or should be classified as "the mission field."

"The one thing the Bible talks about is best described with two words: redemption and missions."

Look again at the definition of missions in the previous paragraph. The "you" of the Old Testament is the nation of Israel. In instituting the nation of Israel, God told Abraham, "I will make you into a great nation . . . and all peoples on earth will be blessed *through you*" (Gen. 12:2, 3 NIV). Commenting on this encounter between Abraham and God, the New Testament tells us, "The promises were spoken to Abraham and to his seed. Scripture does not say 'and to seeds,' meaning many people, but 'and to your seed,' meaning one person, who is Christ" (Gal. 3:16, NIV). God chose Israel so that through Israel He could bring Christ to the world. That's missions. God didn't choose Israel as an end in itself but as a means to the end of bringing Jesus Christ to the world.

---

> "Redemption is God's work of bringing Jesus Christ to a world who needs Him."

---

The "you" of the New Testament then is the church of Jesus Christ, or all true believers. Just as God in the Old Testament told Abraham, "I will make you into a great nation" (Gen. 12:2, NIV), so God the Son, Jesus, told His disciples, "I will build my church" (Matt. 16:18). Speaking to the believers in the New Testament, Peter says, "But you are a chosen people . . . that you may declare the praises of him who called you out of darkness into his wonderful light" (1 Pet. 2:9, NIV). God chose the church so that through the church He could bring Christ to the world. That's missions. God didn't choose the church as an end in itself but as a means to the end of bringing Jesus Christ to the world.

Let's take this one step further and make it personal. While it is true that God chose Israel and the church so that through them He could bring Jesus Christ to the world, it is also true that God chose you so that through you He could bring Jesus Christ to the world. Jesus, God the Son, says to His disciples, "You did not choose me, but I chose you and appointed you so that you might *go* and bear fruit—fruit that will last" (John 15:16, NIV). God didn't choose us and save us as an end in itself but as a means to the end of bringing Jesus Christ to a lost world. We all need to be intentionally involved in God's world-wide plan of redemption and missions—the one thing the Bible talks about.

One of the great missionary-sending churches in recent decades is the Virginia Beach Community Chapel in Virginia Beach, Virginia. Written in large letters across one entire wall of that church's sanctuary building are these words, "THE WORLD IS ON GOD'S HEART." It's a great missionary slogan; is it true? Twice in the New Testament Jesus said, "Out of the abundance of the heart the mouth speaks" (Matt. 12:34; Luke 6:45), meaning that what we say reveals who we really are. What comes out of our mouths shows what is really in our hearts. Not only does that truth apply to us; it also applies to God. What God says reveals what is on God's heart; and from Genesis to Revelation, the "mouth" of God as seen in His Word has been revealing His heart for a lost and dying world.

There are two interesting passages of Scripture where the Holy Spirit draws back the curtain of time and allows us to listen in on the eternal conversation of the Godhead: Isaiah 6 and John 17. In Isaiah 6, the prophet Isaiah has a vision of the triune God ("Holy, holy, holy") and hears God saying, "Whom shall I send, and who will go for us?" (Isa. 6:8). God the Father, Son and Holy Spirit is conversing with Himself. What He says reveals what is on His heart, which is lost people in need of His love and forgiveness, as well as the need for someone to go to them with that message. In John 17, Jesus is praying to His Father just before going to the cross. Here again we are given a chance to listen in on the eternal conversation of the Godhead as God the Son speaks to God the Father. The word "world" occurs eighteen times in the twenty-six verses of John 17. During His prayer, the Son says to the Father, "As you sent me into the world, so I have sent them into the world" (John 17:18). When God speaks to God, it is obvious that the world is on His heart. As we, individually and as local churches, walk closely with the Lord, the whole world should be on our hearts too.

> "God didn't chose us and save us as an end in itself but as a means to the end of bringing Jesus Christ to a lost world."

People's last words, spoken at the end of their earthly life, usually have great significance. Five times near the end of His earthly life, just before ascending back into heaven, Jesus commissioned us, His church, to take the gospel message to the whole world (see Matt. 28:18–20; Mark 16:15; Luke 24:47–48; John 20:21; Acts 1:8). These five clear commissionings are recorded in Scripture by four human authors—Matthew, Mark, Luke and John. While it's tempting to assume all of these recordings came from the same occasion, a careful study of the context of these five commissionings reveals that they were given on five completely separate occasions. In other words, these aren't just five accounts of something Jesus said once; they are accounts of something Jesus said five different times. Anything that Jesus says even once is important; so when Jesus says the same thing five times, it is *really* important. We are to take the message of the gospel to the whole world. It's not something we *might* do; it's something we *must* do. It's not an option; it's an obligation.

It's clear then that redemption and missions are the one thing the Bible is talking about. It's clear that the whole world is on God's heart. And it's clear that Jesus commissioned us, His church, to take the gospel to the ends of the earth. At this point, we should ask ourselves two questions: What is the gospel? And why do we need to take it to the whole world? The gospel, a word that means "good news," is the message about the person and work of Jesus Christ. This message needs to be taken to the whole world because all have sinned and are under God's just wrath and because there is no other way of salvation apart from Jesus Christ (see John 14:6).

---

"What comes out of our mouths shows
what is really in our hearts."

---

Only Jesus, the perfect, eternal Son of God, could pay the full penalty for sin as demanded by a righteous God (see 2 Cor. 5:21). Only when a sinful person puts his faith in the person and work of Christ will that person be saved, reconciled to God for eternity. This is why Jesus says to us, "Go into all the world and preach the gospel to all creation" (Mark 16:15, NIV). This is not a suggestion; it is a command. In making this statement, Jesus wasn't employing hyperbole like coaches do in the locker room to get their team psyched up before a game. It is our Lord's desire that every man, woman, boy or girl, living anywhere on earth, will have the chance to hear, understand and respond to the message of the gospel. He is not willing that any should perish (see Ezek. 18:23; 2 Pet. 3:9). He wants all people to be saved and to come to the knowledge of the truth of the gospel (see 1 Tim. 2:1–6). Yet right now there are over two billion people still waiting to hear about Jesus for the first time. For these people, the Bible is an unknown book, the cross is an unknown symbol, and Christmas and Easter are unknown holidays. While we wait joyfully for the second coming of Christ, these people have still never heard of His first coming!

> "Missionaries don't just go to the lost and unreached;
> they are sent to the lost and unreached."

Missionaries don't just go to the lost and unreached; they are sent to the lost and unreached. In fact, the English word "missionary" is derived from the Latin words *missio* (which means "a sending") and *mittere* (which means "to send"). While the word "missionary" does not occur in most English translations of the Bible, the word "apostle" does. The English word "apostle" is derived from the Greek words *apo* (which means "from") and *stello* (which means "to send"), so it is not wrong to say that the words "missionary" and "apostle" are synonymous. (While the title "apostle" seems to be specifically used in the New Testament to denote the twelve men who had accompanied Christ throughout His earthly ministry and were eyewitnesses of Christ's resurrection, the word "apostle" is also used more widely to describe all who were missionaries including Paul, Barnabus, Adronicus, Junia, Epaphroditus, Silas and Timothy.) Interestingly, Jesus Himself is called "the apostle [missionary] . . . whom we confess" (Heb. 3:1, NIV 1984), which fits perfectly with the numerous times in the New Testament where Jesus says that He was "sent" to a lost world by His Father. In fact, Jesus takes this a logical step further when He says to His disciples: "As the Father has sent [*apo-stello*] me, even so I am sending you" (John 20:21).

A missionary, then, is a "sent one," and, more specifically, a "sent from" one. But sent from where to where? Missionary sending is not a haphazard sending from anywhere to anywhere; it is a deliberate sending from where the gospel is known to where the gospel is not known. It is a sending from where people do know about Jesus to where people don't and won't know about Jesus unless someone goes to them with the message of the gospel.

The question remains: If missionaries are "sent ones," by whom are they sent? The first and obvious answer is that missionaries are sent to a lost world by the Lord Himself. Jesus says, "As the Father has sent me, even so I am sending you" (John 20:21). In the Old Testament, God says, "Whom shall I send, and who will go for us?"

(Isa. 6:8). Our God is a missionary-sending God, but it is equally true to say that missionaries are sent by the local church. This can be seen from a careful study of the first few verses of Acts 13, where the local church at Antioch selects and sends out Paul and Barnabas on their first missionary journey. In his book *Luke: Historian and Theologian*, scholar I. Howard Marshall makes a convincing case that Luke, penning his Gospel and the book of Acts under the inspiration of the Holy Spirit, was writing with didactic intent and not just to record history.[1]

In the opening verses of Acts 13, as the leadership of the local church in Antioch are worshiping and fasting, God speaks directly to them, the church leaders, and tells them to set apart Barnabas and Saul (later named Paul) for missionary service. In all fairness to the text, it says that the local church leaders are to identify and set apart Barnabas and Saul "for the work to which I have called them." The phrase "to which I have called them" could mean that Barnabas and Saul had previously sensed the Lord's call to them directly (and perhaps shared that sense of calling with the church leaders) and that the Lord was now confirming that call to the church leaders. Or it could mean that Barnabas and Saul were receiving their call initially from the Lord via the praying church leaders. Either way, whether initiated or simply recognized by the church leaders, the leadership of the local church is an important part of God's missionary sending. In other words, Barnabas and Paul don't strike out on their own, apart from the prayerful confirmation of their local church leaders. Sadly, more

than one missionary for whom I have been responsible has refused to do what his or her local church
leadership requested and instructed, instead stating,
"God has told me directly what I am to do." Interestingly, Acts 13 tells us that Barnabas and Saul were
sent out both by the church and by God. In Acts 13:3 it
says the local church leaders "sent them off." Yet Acts
13:4 says the two missionaries were "sent out by the
Holy Spirit." There is no contradiction here. We are
told that Barnabas and Saul were sent out as missionaries by God, and that He carried out that sending via
the recognition and confirmation of the leadership of
the local church.

> "... right now there are over two billion people still waiting
> to hear about Jesus for the first time."

When my wife and I went to Italy as church-planting missionaries, we were sent out by a wonderful and
supportive local church. While several other churches
and individuals financially supported our missionary
work, we only had one home sending church. We met
all the requirements to be official members of that local
church. I was ordained to the gospel ministry under the
examination and leadership of a ministerial council as-
sembled by that local church; we served in a variety of
ministry roles within that church before ever proceeding
to the mission field; our local church leadership helped
us to find a bona fide missionary agency with whom we

could serve, an agency that provided competent on-field supervision; and we were officially "commissioned" for missionary service by the leaders of that church and in the presence of the entire congregation. While we were on the mission field, our local sending church kept in constant contact with us and with our mission agency, both for support and accountability. When I was asked to become the leader of the missionary agency with whom we had been serving for thirteen years as missionaries, we made the decision to move back to North America and take the position only after consulting with our sending church and receiving confirmation from its leadership. In fact, our local sending church insisted on having a congregational commissioning service, during which they prayed for us and publicly showed their approval of this new chapter in our missionary service. How awesome is that? Our local sending church continued to support us financially and in prayer over the next seventeen years, during which we were involved in missions leadership and administration.

> "It is exciting and sobering for those who sense a call to missionary service to realize that they are not 'on their own.'"

It is exciting and sobering to realize that we, as local churches, have the God-given privilege and responsibility to send missionaries to the unreached peoples of the world. It is exciting and sobering for those who sense a call to missionary service to realize that they are not "on their own," but can and should have the confirmation, support and accountability provided by a local sending church.

# 3

## THE BLESSING OF SENDING
### HOW IS IT PERSONAL AND ENERGIZING?

S ending is a transformative experience for everyone involved. It stimulates the local church to think
globally. Sending encourages incarnational living
and serving. It is a unique, life-changing way in which a
church can offer itself to the world. Sending is a powerful way to personalize the Great Commission corporately and individually.

Those who are sent are changed and stretched by
the varied circumstances they encounter. Every day can
bring new acquaintances as well as fresh sets of prob-
lems. Challenges, combined with teachability before
God, result in growth and blessing.

The people among whom missionaries are sent to
live also change. As their world broadens through the
presence of people from a different culture with a different language and different ideas, they reevaluate their
stereotypes of outsiders. The whole point of a sending
ministry is to give others the opportunity to hear and respond to the gospel.

The sending church is changed, along with its missionaries and the people they impact. Doss Estep, the former Minister of Missions at Urbancrest Baptist Church, said, "When God leads everyday people out of a church to other parts of the world, everyone's perspective of the world and God's mission changes. The biblical mandate and the Spirit of God will direct and transform churches through it. This is the fuel of the church."[1]

---

"The whole point of a sending ministry is to give others the opportunity to hear and respond to the gospel."

---

In choosing to participate in reaching all nations, the sending church steps into a potentially transformational experience. The example set by those sent, as well as their willingness to embrace a completely new life in a challenging part of the world, provokes both admiration and self-evaluation on the part of their senders. The challenge to sustain the financial and ministry efforts of the sent ones is also transformational. In his book *Loving the Church . . . Blessing the Nations: Pursuing the Role of Local Churches in Global Mission*, George Miley points out: "Missions offers a God-sized challenge in which our lives can be meaningfully and joyfully invested. It provides for our God-given need for significance. It can absorb all of our creativity. Missionary or non-missionary, it doesn't matter. Everyone has a place at the table."[2] Sending is a powerful experience. It can build a unique sense of teamwork within the church as people unite to participate in reaching the unreached.

There are many ways sending can bless the life of the local church. First, it stimulates the local church to cultivate a global focus. The North American church has become a self-absorbed entity, spending a great deal of time, staff effort and resources on what happens within churches' facilities. Joel Holm has observed, "The church has tried to flourish by focusing mainly on areas of ministry directly related to its own community life, rather than on its mission."[3] A brief study of church budgets exposes the discrepancies between local and worldwide ministry focus. However, when a local body sends out a member from the fellowship to a cross-cultural ministry, a unique linkage is established. The place where the member goes is no longer just a place on the map. A part of the church body is now present in another area of the world, and with them goes not just a monetary investment but an emotional one as well. This draws those in the sending church into that ministry and mission field.

When we were living in Michigan, our two daughters chose to attend a Christian college in Mississippi. We had never had any contact with that school before our oldest daughter chose to go there. We'd never even been in that state. However, before we left her there, we learned about the history and values of the college—and about its surrounding community. We became emotionally invested in the place that would be her home for the next few years. We returned to our home, and she began a journey into a new culture and life experiences that enriched her academically and spiritually. As "senders," we grew spiritually as we launched her, and then her sister, on this journey. This was a life-changing move, not only for our daughter but for us as well. By the time our second daughter joined our first at the same college, we had become close friends with members of a church in that town. This friendship opened opportunities for us to encourage these new friends in their desire to be more invested in global outreach. When we sent our daughter, we sent part of our family. Although it cost us to send some of our financial and many of our prayer resources with her, we knew that sending her and her sister to this college was brought about by God. In a similar way, sending churches also become aware that God has orchestrated the relocation of some of their church members. This is often God's way of getting a church to adopt a cross-cultural focus. This is a providential event for the whole church; as a result, there is potential for developing a meaningful ministry connection. This is literally a God-given opportunity for every person to impact a small part of the world together.

In discussing the expansion of the church, Joel Holm states, "The local church is not just called to support the construction. It is called to build."[4] Sending out missionaries uniquely positions the church to build. Regardless of the length of the missions assignment, there is considerable potential for congregational impact. Someone sent out for two years will undergo an extensive life reorientation. If that person communicates their experiences and personal growth to the sending church, it often challenges many within the body. If the sending relationship is not short-term but is stretched over a lifetime, the shared insights enrich everyone involved. It is not just the sent ones who have maturing life experiences; senders also face challenges and lessons that shape them. Even the act of financially supporting someone by faith can draw a congregation into greater dependency on God.

### "Everyone has a place at the table."

When reviewing the sending relationship, one can easily identify practical ways to link people together to facilitate missions. Short-term ministry trips can bring people from a variety of backgrounds together to partner with missionaries. The period of preparation and dedicated times of prayer will intensify the unity of purpose among participants as they realize that they are part of something with eternal results. Carefully planned trips can aid missionaries in practical ways, while informing the participants about another culture and ministry. Upon the return of the team, a special reentry effort can leverage the growth of individuals for long-term impact in the church.

Another practical way to link the people at home with the people sent out is the creation of a prayer tool. Wide circulation of this resource can help maintain prayer support and interest in the ministry. Many today utilize technology like Skype to stimulate a bond with the missionary or national coworkers. We are now able to call halfway around the world to talk and pray with our people at very little expense. When missionaries are back for home assignment, they can reenter the activities of the church, fostering new contacts and invigorating the church's connection to the people among whom they have been ministering. One of the most ready-made ways for a church to develop ministry friendships overseas is through the ones they have sent, whether through the missionary or through those from the sending church who visit the missionary and participate in their work.

> "Even the act of financially supporting someone
> by faith can draw a congregation
> into greater dependency on God."

A second way in which sending can bless the life of the local church is as a tutorial experience of incarnational serving. Simply put, we have the opportunity to develop a willingness to replace our preferences with a sacrificial love for Christ and the lost. Today's church is often described as self-centered and materialistic. A focus on church campus growth to the neglect of global impact will not shape the character of the church the way God intended. When missionaries come face-to-face with people unlike themselves, they evaluate how to relate to them and be accepted. This is not a matter of living a compromised life to win favor. Instead, it is a choice to cultivate insight into who the people are and how to express God's love to them. Those in cross-cultural ministry know how critical it is to gain an audience for the gospel, which may include surrendering one's rights and preferences so that those without Christ can be reached. Both the sent ones and the senders should emulate this lifestyle. Imagine a coordinated effort, with people from the sending church joining the missionary overseas to implement incarnational ministry efforts. These people can help with a project and, for a short time, experience daily living abroad as they bond with both the missionary and the mission. Before the team returns home, they and the missionary meet together to talk about what they have learned about themselves, the ministry and God. With agency help, this holds potential for life change and long-term results. This addresses the assumption by some that only missionaries are expected to live a life of surrender, and it provides another opportunity for the senders to enter true fellowship with those sent. John Stott talks about the incarnational lifestyle this way: "It tells us that mission involves being under the authority of Christ (we are sent, we did not volunteer); renouncing privilege, safety, comfort and aloofness, as we actually enter other people's worlds, as he entered ours; humbling ourselves to become servants, as he did."[5] This type of shared experience can deeply enrich our lives. Craig Ott, Stephen J. Strauss and Timothy C. Tennent add, "The church must never cease to learn the value of ministry shaped by the attitude of Christ and guided by the Pauline principle of 'all things to all men that I may by all means win some.'"[6]

We all need to be lifelong learners. When the topic of sending surfaces, sometimes through the occasional guest speaker, people tend to cerebrally dissect the concept rather than step out in faith and experience all God has in store for them individually and for the church corporately. The sending experience can be a very stretching and worthwhile period of learning. In order for the church to have a sense of partnership with the one sent, the two must have frequent opportunities to communicate. For example, the sending church and those they sent might keep contact through blogging to stay together on their journey.

Sent ones learn, or have learned, that sorting through character issues directly relates to building redemptive relationships. The qualities of unconditional love, humility, servanthood and sacrifice need to be present in all our daily relationships. We need more life-on-life transparency and sharing. Sending can be an effective tool to provoke this deeper spiritual life.

There is a third way that sending can bless the life of the church. When a local church sends, it offers, or should offer, itself in a special way to the world. The sending church affirms, supports and sustains the sent ones in many practical and personal ways. The sending church offers itself to serve the community where the missionary has been sent.

In addition to these relationships, the church also develops and nurtures connections with other churches. A church with a passion to see the nations reached with the gospel can offer itself as a tutorial for sending. This is to be done in the same spirit of servanthood evidenced in the lives of those sent. The sending church's missionary may have been in contact with other stateside churches before going overseas. Members of the sending church can utilize their passion and abilities to assist other local churches to develop their sending capacities.

A church with experience in sending can balance a less experienced church's enthusiasm with practical guidance, especially regarding the need to be careful about security concerns. Through electronic communications or prayer bulletins, an inexperienced church might inadvertently put their missionary in danger. A church with more experience can apprise them of safer ways to communicate with and about their missionary.

> "There is a large harvest waiting for workers."

The point is that shared ministry and appropriate influence should always be prayerfully explored. This is an ideal time for the missionary, agency and church to collaborate toward a more unified vision for a region overseas. While attempting to assist in the work, the church can know the beauty of ministry friendships.

The church can offer itself to the world through a relationship with the national church. Believers can go as learners and servants, applying the incarnational lifestyle in the context of friendship. Direct or indirect involvement, conducted humbly and lovingly, should be motivated by the desire to honor Christ. The church should not consider any good work as being beneath them.

Building an incarnational lifestyle in the church requires real adjustment. Churches today are full of people who are accustomed to being in charge. Many live a very sanitized lifestyle and are even germophobic. We must evaluate our willingness to serve and our ability to exercise flexibility within a wide variety of circumstances.

---

## "We need more life-on-life transparency and sharing."

---

How much do we really care about offering ourselves to the world? The sending church creates natural linkage for broader ministry overseas, but we must prepare ourselves to identify with the rest of the world. We must be willing to get our hands dirty. We must surrender our comfortable lives to God.

It is always helpful for a church to evaluate where it is regarding the blessing of sending. I always asked two questions. First, what have we offered to God to intentionally contribute to making disciples of all nations? There are a wide variety of appropriate answers. Second, whom have we offered to God to intentionally contribute toward making disciples of all nations? These questions begin to personalize the Great Commission challenge for us all. Tom Julien lends a helpful perspective in sharing: "Pastor Smith sat silent. Until now he had been concerned about getting people of the world into the church. But he had shown little or no concern about getting people of the church into the world. The church had gradually become a basin rather than a base, a collection agency rather than a sending agency. He had seen the people as plants to be watered rather than seeds to be planted."[7] In Matthew 9:37, we learn that there is a shortage of laborers to bring in the harvest. We are instructed to pray for more laborers to be sent out. The struggle this verse addresses is the lack of workers to bring in the harvest. We all need to reflect on how we ourselves can remedy the shortage.

There is a large harvest waiting for workers. Pat Hood writes: "God is a sending God. The greatest example is God sending His Son to be a cross-cultural missionary on planet earth. But there are plenty of other sending examples in the Bible. From Abraham to Moses to Paul to you, God's people are always being sent into the world on a mission."[8] Is your church willing to be a participant in this mission?

### Action Points

1. How would you assess your church's present global focus? Nonexistent? Weak? Growing? Strong? How do you respond to the statement: "The local church is not just called to support construction; it is called to build"?

2. What are some practical ways your church can develop a personal connection with an overseas missionary?

3. How can your church utilize sending as a tutorial experience for incarnational serving? How can you encourage life-on-life sharing?

4. How might your local church offer itself to the world?

# PART 2

## OWNING THE CHURCH'S SPECIAL PATH

# 4

# THE MOBILIZATION KEYS
## WHAT CAN FORTIFY THE CHURCH?

Sending can infuse the local church with a new vitality. In order to begin that journey, we need to examine the characteristics that are critical to developing a strong sending environment. Every church should fortify itself for sending. This journey will develop faith, resiliency and confidence within that local body of believers. As a high view of God becomes normative in a local church, its members respond to the Great Commission's call to action.

Allow me to introduce the Standard family. Mr. and Mrs. Standard attend Shepherd Community Church. They raised their now-adult children in Shepherd Community Church. Although Shepherd Community Church is not perfect, there is a great deal to admire about its ministry. About six months ago, an outside speaker challenged the congregation to take the gospel to the ends of the earth. One of the Standard children was greatly impacted by the message. He told others about his desire to explore what going overseas with his family might look like. Immediately, his parents became concerned. What about his great college education? Why would he leave the security of home to enter a dangerous and unpredictable world? Was it even realistic to uproot his family and think that he could adequately support them overseas? His parents reasoned that there was a lot of important work to be done right in their community.

> "Sending can infuse the local church
> with a new vitality."

When the parents expressed their nervousness to their son, he thought their concerns sounded more like objections. The son's exploration process became more complicated than he had originally expected. The church leaders floundered in their ability to help this young family since it had been a long time since they had sent anyone overseas. The son began to wonder if his parents had a point. The Standard family was in need of a church that was prepared to address their questions.

We all know that scenarios like this happen fairly frequently in many good churches. In *Here to There: Getting from CROSS to Your Mission Field*, David Meade writes that many start on a serious exploration of overseas service but never end up going. "More than 8 out of 10 missionary candidates fail to get to the field. Many intend to go; few make it."[1] The statistics show how common it is for a candidate to never make it overseas. There is a great deal at stake here.

In order for an individual or family to move into a cross-cultural exploration mode, something should have already happened—the local church should have already gone on a preparatory journey. In attempting to engage a complicated and needy world, the church should fortify itself for a potential sending role. Here is the question every church should ask: How do we prepare ourselves to be a sending church in a way that is both workable for us and meaningful for the person inquiring about missions? Although moving into the unknown can be daunting, careful planning and church-wide convictions overcome the downfalls of inexperience and help lead the way forward. If Shepherd Community Church had been fortified, the Standard family could have had a rich, meaningful experience.

I have found four basic ingredients that, regardless of a church's culture, size or circumstance, are vital to making it a healthy sending church. The first ingredient is the message that is conveyed by the church on a weekly basis. A church needs to reflect on these questions:

- Is the message consistent across all age-groups?
- What does the message encourage more—risk aversion or implicit trust in God?
- Does the body understand what walking in faith looks like?
- Are Christ's lordship and its implications understood?
- Is there a biblical understanding of fulfillment and success?

- What do church members believe are legitimate and illegitimate motivations in life?
- What picture of God is gained through the ministry?

Some may think issues like these have no correlation to sending, but they do. These topics, and more, are fully informed by one factor—a high view of God. Every local church needs to communicate a high view of God, which results in understanding and reflecting God's character and heart. When this takes place in the church, anything can happen. Anglican minister J.B. Phillips writes, "The trouble with many people today is that they have not found a God big enough for modern needs. . . . Too many of us are crippled by a limited idea of God."[2] Who, young or old, would ever consider going to the ends of the earth unless he or she worshiped and served an all-knowing, all-powerful God?

> "In attempting to engage a complicated and needy world, the church should fortify itself for a potential sending role."

As a high view of God becomes normative in a local church, the members respond to the Great Commission's call to action. The church begins to see the world as God sees it and more readily follows God into the unknown. I do not believe it is possible to completely eliminate all our fears and anxiety when we follow God, lest we become self-sufficient rather than God-dependent. A high view of God, rooted in the Scriptures, can enable us to respond to the command to make disciples of all nations. Given this, was Shepherd Community Church prepared to help the Standard family discover whether or not they should go overseas? Who should be required to provide answers to this question?

The second mobilization ingredient to fortifying the church is having role models. Churches should ask whether living examples of missions are available within their community. For example, a missions coach or advocate who is further along on the journey toward cross-cultural ministry could encourage and guide the Standard family. Churches should ask whether there are potential role models in their congregations. These would include people (both young and old) who are passionate, globally thinking Christians and cross-cultural missionaries. In his book *How to Be a World-Class Christian: Becoming Part of God's Global Kingdom*, Paul Borthwick describes a world-class Christian as "one whose lifestyle and obedience are compatible, in cooperation and in accord with what God is doing and wants to do in our world."[3] People of this caliber greatly enhance the perspective of others around them. Those who have taken personal ownership of the Great Commission—who pray, give, send and go—will impact others. Providing opportunities for such people to have influence does not happen by accident, but church leadership can intentionally orchestrate meaningful fellowship. It is vital to identify these individuals in a congregation or area, with the aim of leveraging their potential. They are ready-made vision carriers, providentially placed by God.

Some may say that no such person exists within their church body. If this is true, then the first step is to identify and develop people who can exert influence. Expand the ranks! Single out two or three people who have potential, and explain to them the need to shepherd individuals through various phases of missions interest and involvement. Here is a short list of helpful activities to further develop those individuals:

- Deploy them overseas. Upon reentry, provide tools for an ongoing growth process.
- Facilitate their interaction with similar people from other churches or organizations.
- Guide them to discover local cross-cultural friendships and experiences.
- Take them through good Bible study material on missions.
- Hire them to be on the ministry staff.
- Pray for their direction in identifying and building friendships.
- Provide missions elective classes to help identify interested individuals.
- Contact a few mission agencies with similar vision and values to request role models.

Mission-agency personnel, typically called mobilizers, can visit a church several times a year to present ministry opportunities and to interact with and encourage a variety of audiences. They inform others about how God is at work in the world. They can help implement special events. They can teach a crash course on missions over a weekend. They can stimulate others to dream about how God wants to use the local church to make a real difference in another, specific part of the world. The result of their influence is evident when God's heart for the world becomes more prominent within the church.

---

> "The church begins to see the world as God sees it and more readily follows God into the unknown."

---

Agency mobilizers should seek to work in concert with church mobilizers; and they may be in an ideal position to help equip volunteers within the church who can, in turn, mobilize others. A helpful definition of a mobilizer's job is given by the Center for Mission Mobilization in *Go Mobilize*: "to engage, equip and connect believers—and churches—worldwide to their most strategic role in fulfilling the Great Commission."[4] Two additional resources for mobilizers by CMM Press are *Xplore* and *Coaching Conversations for Mobilizers*.[5] Mobilizers can ask, "How can God's heart for the world become more prominent in my life and in the life of my church?" Answers to this question form the basis for training potential mobilizers.

The third ingredient that fortifies the church is developing the financial capacity to send. Although money should never be the determining factor in ministry planning, lest it deprive the church of walking by faith, the reality is that sending people requires money. Physically relocating people overseas for incarnational ministry comes with a price tag. When challenged to begin sending, a church's first objection is usually the fiscal challenge it presents. We are called, however, to walk by faith and not by sight, not only as individuals but also as churches and mission agencies. If sending is seen as important, the church will develop the ability to trust God's plans at a financial level. It is intriguing and exciting to watch churches succeed in making this happen. The following examples demonstrate a few unique methods churches have adopted.

- Over the years, some churches have constructed consortiums, groups of like-minded churches that help support one another's missionary candidates. The sending church contributes a larger prearranged amount of monthly support. All other churches assume lesser amounts, yet all make a monthly financial commitment to the candidate. This facilitates establishing a full support base for candidates, while also making it possible for them to be launched more quickly.

- Churches can be intentional about expanding their ministry by consistently designating a line item in the annual budget for "Proposed New Support." In this way, they build support in advance, so they're ready to send as soon as a candidate is ready to go.

- Several years ago, I became acquainted with a church that challenged people to give one dollar a day for missions. This may not sound like much of a commitment, but if only fifty people in a church of any size agreed to this, $1,500 in monthly support would be realized. The economy of scale does wonders. On one occasion, I had a family approach me to ask how much they should give to missions. This doesn't happen very often. I noticed that they had a family cell phone plan, evidently for both communications and entertainment, and I suggested that they consider giving to missions an amount equal to the monthly cost of their plan. Operating by this same principle, each can determine an appropriate level of giving by assessing what is most valuable to them.

- While serving in our church in West Michigan, we became aware of another method of financial planning, thanks to our ministry focus in Ukraine. When we sent short-term teams to Ukraine, we always requested that the receiving church provide an equal number of their people to work with ours. On one occasion, a church was finding it difficult to secure the volunteer help needed; so one Sunday, the pastor divided the congregation into several parts and explained that one part would volunteer to work on Monday and the next on Tuesday and so forth. I discovered that volunteers are hard to find within any culture! During previous visits, I had a hard time persuading church leaders in Ukraine that they should support and send out missionaries. They had been on the receiving end for more than five years and repeatedly stated that it was easy for Americans to send because they have money. When I saw this Ukrainian pastor's method of recruiting volunteers, God gave us an answer for sending. We explained that the Ukrainian church or churches could divide into twelve parts. Each part would assume one month of missionary support and would have an entire year to save or work for that one month of support. We suggested that they gather financial support to send workers in the same way that they secured volunteers. It is important to note that this area of Ukraine had an unemployment rate of over 50% at the time; but from that point on, they never again saw sending as impossible.

Most of us will readily admit that sending capacity is really a matter of priorities. Many Western believers have spent much of their adult lives building personal financial resources for their dreams, a rainy day or retirement. We have seldom brought this healthy practice of saving into the church. Why not put our financial expertise to work in a new way?

The fourth ingredient needed to fortify the church is developing advocacy among church leaders. What a difference it would have made for the Standard family if their leadership had perceived the exploration process as exciting rather than stressful! It is important to understand that most key leaders in our churches are extremely busy and are already being pulled in many directions.

Missions enthusiasts may need to adjust their expectations when it comes to leadership involvement. "Developing advocacy" means building a public endorsement of missions in the church and integrating this emphasis into the life of the congregation. This does not mean that church leadership adds missions to their to-do list. It means that they will encourage and resource others to champion the missions cause. In Latin America, it is often said that when it comes to missions in the church, the pastor either holds the key to the front door or holds the padlock. This is true in a variety of places and cultures. As suggested below, there are strategies that can encourage the pastor or church leadership to hold the key rather than the padlock.

- The first approach to encouraging pastors to be missions-minded is to bring in people from outside of the immediate ministry context who can articulate the cause of missions. A guest speaker or resource person should have some type of personal or small-group interaction with church leadership as well as the congregation. Expertise, supplied relationally, can build deeper appreciation for the cause.

- The second approach is to urge leadership to go overseas. Agencies can facilitate meaningful firsthand experience, and a savings plan or special offering can place this within reach. On occasion, agencies allow missionaries to add a small mobilization line item to their monthly support structure, which make it possible for a church leader to travel overseas at least every other year. Interaction with the body of Christ overseas is extremely beneficial for everyone. I recall traveling overseas with a pastoral staff associate and engaging in a teaching ministry together. When we returned, he made this statement to the congregation, "I know some of you think we'll be hearing about this trip for the next three months. Well, you are wrong. Try the next year and three months!" The trip really deepened his appreciation for the importance of cross-cultural ministry.

---

*"Missions enthusiasts may need to adjust their expectations when it comes to leadership involvement."*

---

- A third approach is to use relationships and events to shape thinking. Agencies and mobilizers can suggest unique missions events for individuals in the church to attend, such as visiting a Perspectives class (perspectives.org) following a meal together. The church could also hold special events that stimulate thinking about countries in the news or persecution or disaster relief, all conducted with the intent of fostering relevant involvement.

- A fourth approach is to reveal God's heart for the world through the study of the Scriptures. Multiple materials are available today and are applicable to many settings, from a small-group meeting in a home to a missions elective class on a Sunday. Facilitating an elective can be as simple as playing a DVD for a group that includes key decision makers.

- A fifth approach to building advocacy among leaders is to learn to deliver persuasive arguments. The right DVD or website can assist with this, while statistics or graphs properly presented may provide a fresh, compelling perspective. Incisive questions that invite responses include: When was the last time your church sent out one of its own members overseas? What can you learn from your own local church history? Are there any areas in which your church has grown comfortable or stagnant?

- A sixth approach is to ask for help and direction from leadership. Establish missions goals and work together to construct a timeline for accomplishing these goals. Organize a brainstorming session with other like-minded individuals to generate ideas and ask, "What would be our faith response to the ideas or needs presented?" Include leadership in planning to bring people together and nurture ownership of the ministry. Always plan well in advance and be prepared to use everyone's time wisely.

- The seventh approach is to pray regularly for church leadership. Pray that each one remains teachable. Pray for God to impress upon the church the very real needs of the world and how to respond to them. If any church were to fortify itself for a sending process, what would be the implications for the "Standard family" in that congregation and for the church as a whole?

## Action Points

1. Three of the four ingredients for healthy sending are a high view of God, role models and building financial capacity. Which one of these needs more attention in your church right now? What are some things that can be done to effect improvement in that area?

2. In order to build advocacy among church leaders, identify two of the seven approaches to follow up on now. Who will own the action, and what steps will this involve?

# 5

# THE MOBILIZATION ROLE
## HOW DOES THE CHURCH CONTRIBUTE?

I n order to send people to the nations, a church needs to know the role it should play. This will be a process that prepares the church and the individual or couple for a lifetime of ministry together. It is a time for both missionary and partnership development.

There are four basic building blocks a church can introduce to every missionary candidate. A church of virtually any size can provide basic training, functioning as a dynamic learning laboratory. The church can make its own unique contribution by developing competencies in its people.

When we unpack Acts 13:1–3, we discover how we can become more fully engaged in sending. This sending experience for the church in Antioch was not random. It was quite intentional due to God's involvement. In *The Imitation of Saint Paul: Examining Our Lives in Light of His Example*, Jim Reapsome states, "This initial mission of the church did not originate with the church but with

God."[1] The Holy Spirit made certain that this specific part of the plan—sending—was in synchronization with all that the Godhead had previously intended and commanded. Reapsome says of Antioch, "Their story stands as a model of all subsequent Christian missionary enterprise. Mission must be Spirit induced and church encouraged and supported."[2] The local church is to follow this synchronized, Spirit-induced ministry model and become active in sending.

---

**The church can make its own unique contribution by developing competencies in its people.**

---

There are many potential implications for ministry today in light of this first sending event. Reflect on Acts 13 and on the church of today. Now consider this question that a ministry friend of mine often asks: Are churches today really sending, or are missionaries simply going? To fully answer this question, we will more thoroughly analyze the passage.

In this text, it appears that when the Holy Spirit calls an individual within the church, He calls the church to action as well. It is also important to recognize that all of the church leadership was placed under the Spirit's notification about the specifics of who to send. They all laid hands on Barnabas and Saul and then sent them into missionary service. There is nothing passive here. The leadership gave evidence that they all shared this interest and commitment. By the laying on of hands, they publically endorsed this call and affirmed their co-workers, becoming symbolically and practically bound together to a common ministry. Our churches today must ask: What does it mean today to be bound together emotionally? Financially? Logistically? Spiritually? What might this look like in our sending process? If the Holy Spirit calls both the individual and the church to action, what form would this take? In some basic way, we should be bound together.

Missions leaders over the years have looked at Acts 13 and Third John 5–8, among other passages, to emphasize that the local church body should see itself as a partner in the truth with missionaries. This partnership has resulted in the formation of small groups within the body that care for and affirm their missionaries. Some churches refer to these groups as Barnabas Teams. In our church ministry we refer to them as PAC Teams, or Prayer and Care Teams, and each of our overseas workers is required to have a PAC Team. A brochure exemplifying how a PAC Team operates is available in Appendix 2. This has become one expression of being bound together at a grassroots level of member care for workers. The first role of the local church then, both the leadership and the laity, is to become engaged in sending.

The second role is to become engaged in preparing. The laying on of hands is both an endorsement of the people sent and an endorsement of the plan to send. Church leadership had no reservations about sending Barnabas or Saul, even though the Spirit later on records Paul's resistance to John Mark as a possible companion (see Acts 15:37–38). The laying on of hands signified that qualified people were being presented for missionary service, men who were capable of crossing barriers of distance, language and culture to represent Christ and build the church.

> "The laying on of hands is both an endorsement of the people sent and an endorsement of the plan to send."

In the Antioch selection process, the Holy Spirit identified workers who possessed a proven track record. Barnabas and Saul were already "living sent" through their home church. Overseas ministry is not just driven by the subjective experience of a missionary call. Barnabas and Saul had excellent ministry experience (see Acts 11:25–26) as prophets or teachers or both. Additionally, the composition of the Antioch church, including church leadership, was quite multicultural. In *Western Christians in Global Mission: What's the Role of the North American Church?*, Paul Borthwick says, "It featured a multicultural, diverse leadership team that included a Cypriot, a Cyrenian (from modern day Libya), an African and others from various strata of society (Acts 13:1–3)."[3] They must have been discerning about cross-cultural differences (see Acts 11:19–23), and they were launching the church into the Gentile world. It was readily apparent that they were men of prayer as well as men of faith. Barnabas and Saul had many unanswered questions; however, their faith enabled them to move forward to embrace uncharted territory and do something new. Their church was an ideal place of preparation, whether they realized it or not.

> "Overseas ministry is not just driven by the subjective experience of a missionary call."

A church of virtually any size can provide basic training and can function as a dynamic learning laboratory. Plenty of institutions can provide a highly valuable education, yet many of us regard formal education as the nearly exclusive path to preparation. Indeed, educational institutions credential people for ministry, which is a worthwhile step for many. At the same time, the local church can make its own unique contribution by implementing training that focuses on developing competencies in people. Not all educated individuals have acquired ministry proficiency. Allow me to suggest four basic building blocks that help cultivate competency. These are transferable to almost any leadership training opportunity that exists today, and there is no financial price tag to these steps.

The first phase in developing ministry aptitude is personal assessment, aimed at uncovering the strengths and weaknesses of an individual. These questions can be employed to lead discussions with a potential missionary:

1. What spiritual gifts do you possess?
2. Have your gifts been affirmed by others observing you in ministry?
3. What are your strengths and weaknesses?
4. Have you had any Bible training (formal or informal) in doctrine? Apologetics? Inductive Bible study? Evangelism? Discipling?
5. Is your Bible training adequate for an overseas assignment?
6. What does a basic personality test reveal about you?
7. Are you willing to learn from others?
8. What does a personality test reveal about the kind of teammate you will make overseas?
9. What have you taught to or modeled for others?

Assessing potential missionaries is critical to identifying their eventual roles and preparing them for deployment. A better ministry fit makes a better missionary. In recent years, many studies have evaluated missionary attrition, revealing a need for improvement within the sphere of member care. Discovering a better ministry fit for missionaries is often an overlooked step. A good fit increases the duration of ministry for the church, agency and missionary. Churches must remember that missionary candidates are not entirely objective about themselves. The church and the agency need to provide some objectivity when it comes to assessment. Several diagnostic tools are available to help churches. For example, an individual or a church could pay a counselor to conduct an assessment and present the results to the candidate and the church. A onetime fee may save everyone a great deal of heartache and embarrassment later.

A second way of building ministry aptitude is spiritual growth. The disciplines of the Christian life must follow a healthy trajectory. Here are some questions to lead discussions with candidates:

1. Are you presently active in sharing your faith? In what way? If not, are you interested in learning how?
2. Have you equipped others to share their faith?
3. What evidence is there that you genuinely care about others?
4. Are you presently praying for the lost here and overseas?

Traveling on a plane to an appointed place of service does not suddenly change your life. A change of location does not make a missionary. Missionaries bring with them the habits and lifestyle they presently possess.

> "Assessing potential missionaries is critical to identifying their eventual roles and to preparing them for deployment."

Personal Bible study is a critical part of growth. Both a working knowledge of the Word and self-directed Bible study skills are vital to spiritual strength. When people go overseas, they usually relinquish the opportunity to receive in-depth messages on Scripture in an established church setting. Once when my wife and I visited a missionary in an unnamed country, he mentioned upon our arrival how timely our visit was. When I asked him why, he stated that we could all go to church together. What he meant by that comment was that my wife and I were in time to sing, pray and read the Scriptures with his family in their living room. This was their only form of church, because in their city of three-quarters of a million people there were only a handful of believers.

---

### "A change of location does not make a missionary."

---

The bottom line is that devotional habits and Bible study skills need to be strong, as does the discipline of prayer. Laboring in prayer for the ministry is extremely important, and those who are preparing to go should pray just as hard for their ministry as the people who are sending them. Prayer is a personal practice and must be constantly developed. It is crucial for the basic disciplines of the Christian life to be thriving in missionaries' lives.

The third building block is ministry experience. Here are some questions to lead future discussions:

1. How are you developing your gifts and abilities?
2. How are you developing godly interpersonal relationship skills?
3. Have you ever shared the gospel with an unbeliever?
4. Have you taught, equipped or led adults?
5. Are you good at counseling or organizing?
6. Have you discipled anyone?

Agencies can suggest or provide specialized training once the specific ministry context is established. On a cautionary note, no missionary candidate should make any further educational plans unless both the church and the agency agree on this path. Education is time-consuming and expensive and can sometimes become a distraction. Unless others perceive additional education as mission-critical, a candidate is encouraged to wait.

The final building block to enhance qualifications for ministry is mentoring. Church leadership can identify people who are able to effectively mentor a potential missionary. Mentors should be respected and spiritually mature, and it is a good bonus if they have cross-cultural experience. Mentors are to encourage the candidate and should provide godly perspective on life in an atmosphere of confidentiality. When a couple is preparing as candidates, it is best to provide a mentoring couple for them. Mentoring should be intentional, so meeting face-to-face each month is highly beneficial. In order to facilitate deeper discussions, a basic work sheet can be used, such as the one in Appendix 3. As a result of this relationship, a mentor is in a good position to evaluate a candidate's readiness and to make practical suggestions to church or agency leadership regarding future ministry. The book *Connecting: The Mentoring Relationships You Need to Succeed* by Paul Stanley and J. Robert Clinton is a valuable resource; it includes "Ten Commandments for Mentoring" that are extremely practical.[4]

## Action Points

1. What ministry reminders come out of Acts 13:1–3 for you, and why are they important for your church?
2. What might it mean for your church to play a more central role in the practical formation of your missionary candidate?
3. Of the four building blocks of missionary preparation, which is most important for you to implement? Why? How can you move forward in this challenge?

# 6

# THE EVALUATION ROLE
## HOW AND WHY DOES THE CHURCH EVALUATE
## A MISSIONARY CALL?

What is the relationship between an individual's "missionary call" and the local church? Several years ago, I was asked to make contact with a young man to explain to him how we, at our church, practiced missions. He wanted to aggressively pursue cross-cultural ministry overseas. There weren't many men advising him at the time, and he was about to make some very important decisions about missionary service. In our phone conversation, I asked what his church thought about his very detailed plan for the future, since he seemed to have everything figured out. He was puzzled and quickly informed me that guidance for his future was essentially up to him and the Holy Spirit. When I respectfully disagreed, he very firmly stated that it was all about him and the Holy Spirit—and no one else. He explained that he answered to God alone. It was a very American response.

Ultimately, we do answer to God, but we are also answerable to others. What would happen if we were only answerable to God? How would we tangibly measure that accountability? How would our local church, agency personnel or national coworkers function effectively? This adult was treating his subjective thoughts as if they were his fast pass to the mission field. If not properly examined, a potential missionary's "call" can become a license to do anything. Sometimes, when strong personalities proceed this way, the local church isn't certain how to respond. Over the years, I have seen a number of people say and do questionable things under the guise of following God, and people do all kinds of things in the name of religion. Every call or prompting that we believe to be from God should be evaluated thoughtfully and unhurriedly.

When Paul and Barnabas were sent out in Acts 13, everyone in church leadership was placed under the Spirit's notification. The lesson we derive from this is that the local church should be able to recognize and affirm a call in a person's life. The Holy Spirit did not simply inform Barnabas and Saul; He also notified others in positions of authority. If the local church is going to be a part of the team that sends, then the Holy Spirit will also inform church leadership. The Holy Spirit uses different methods, and His timing may vary, but He and church leadership were at the center of sending activity from the very beginning. Jim Reapsome says, "Mystery clouds the mechanics of hearing the Holy Spirit, but probably there was strong consensus that God had spoken. Nevertheless, the voice required verification."[1] The Antioch leadership sought stronger confirmation of the call through fasting and prayer. Only after receiving confirmation did they send off Barnabas and Saul. In *A Biblical Theology of Missions*, George Peters states, "Thus, while the call of Christ comes directly to the individual and there is a sending forth by Christ Himself, a spiritual church will also sense the call either directly or indirectly."[2]

---

"Ultimately, we do answer to God,
but we are also answerable to others."

---

The example of the early church demonstrates that the local church should sense and affirm the call of an individual in preparation for a lifetime partnership of cross-cultural ministry. Through the example of Antioch, we learn that going was never designed to be a solo effort nor a unilateral move of the local church. It is important to realize that the resources of the sending church are far more diverse than money. Ultimately, effective sending relies upon a strong ministry relationship between the sending church and the one sent.

How then does a church recognize and affirm a call? People must genuinely make themselves available to God for ministry before anything significant can take place. A church or agency can recognize the potential for missionary service in a person and express this, but progress comes only after that person becomes available. A fortified church offers a ministry environment in which members sense promptings of the Holy Spirit.

Another topic that needs to be assessed is suitability. It is one thing to be available to God and quite another to be suited for effective overseas ministry. Not every person should serve overseas. In our church ministry, we have extensive church-based missionary training. Those interested in this training must apply and be accepted.

---

"People shouldn't be sent out simply because they are sons or daughters of the church."

---

Before they apply, we explain to them how the training works, and we add that we provide a healthy exit strategy for anyone who begins to question if missions is truly the life direction God has chosen for them. When someone chooses to step aside from the training, we validate his or her willingness to explore the possibility of overseas ministry, and we recognize and celebrate the personal growth that has taken place. We are grateful for the clarity God gives regarding each individual's future. We want to develop missionaries, but we also realize that not everyone should engage in cross-cultural ministry.

Any church can carefully evaluate the suitability of a candidate on the basis of three categories. Areas to consider and questions for further discussions are:

## Character

- Are they honest?
- Are they grace-filled in interpersonal relation-ships?
- Is there evidence of integrity?
- Do they easily forgive?
- Are they reliable?
- Are they teachable?

## Competency

- How helpful are they?
- Can they teach and disciple?
- What do they have a love for?
- Do they devote their gifts and abilities to others? The church? Themselves?
- In what ways do they excel? Where is there a need for their specific abilities?
- Is there evidence that they have a servant's heart?

## Compatibility

- Are they in doctrinal agreement?
- Are they supportive of church leadership?
- Do they embrace the church's ministry philoso-phy? The agency's philosophy?

Some churches or organizations have used a fourth "C" word, which is "Chemistry."[3]

- Do they drain or energize others?
- Do they take initiative?

- Do they work well as part of a team?
- Are they one who unites or divides?

People shouldn't be sent out simply because they are sons or daughters of the church, yet they should be affirmed if they have qualities that would contribute to a healthy and effective ministry. If suitability becomes an issue, then it becomes apparent that the timing or the overall viability of entering overseas ministry should be revisited.

These assessments should not be conducted as an inquisition or in an environment of intense scrutiny.

> "Prayer is a significant part of mobilization as well as training for overseas work."

Churches need to have reasonable expectations, while being honest and discerning. If questions concerning the assessment arise, the church could consider enlisting the aid of an agency. Some agencies have their own assessment plan to help both the individual and the church. Finding what is best for both the candidate and the overseas ministry should be what drives every evaluation. Because missionaries change vocations, leave family and friends, receive monthly support, live in a new culture and pursue new ministry goals, it is important to be reasonably certain they are a good fit for their field before sending them.

One additional and vital role the church should assume is that of intercessor. In our church, we say that prayer is not only important—it is essential. Prayer is a significant part of mobilization as well as training for overseas work. The Scriptures call us to pray and, specifically, to "pray earnestly to the Lord of the harvest to send out laborers into his harvest" (Matt. 9:38). George Murray considers the challenge behind these words:

> Jesus says that if we pray he will "send out" workers into the harvest fields of the world. The Greek word translated "send out" in Matthew 9:38 is the same word used in John 2 when Jesus entered the temple in Jerusalem and was outraged by the mercenary, self-seeking commerce of the money changers and dove sellers. On that occasion, we are not told that Jesus asked those merchants to voluntarily leave the temple; instead, we read that He made a physical whip, and with that whip He "drove out" the moneychangers and dove sellers. They could not stay; they had to go. This I believe, is what will happen in the hearts and minds of believers when their church leaders get serious about "praying earnestly" for the need of more workers to be sent to the mission fields of the world. The compelling hand of God will come upon people in such a way that they will not be able to stay; they will have to go, by their own admission.
>
> The same Greek word that is translated "send out" in Matthew 9:38 is used in the New Testament every time Jesus "cast out" an evil spirit. Evil spirits did not come out of people voluntarily; they were compelled to leave because of God's mighty hand coming upon them and thrusting them out. Jesus is saying that He will compulsively move people out to the mission fields of the world if, in earnest prayer, we ask Him to do so. It is interesting to note that on one occasion,

the disciples of Jesus sought to cast out a demon from a young boy but could not do so. Jesus came along and cast the demon out after their failure to do so. When His disciples asked Him how He could cast out the demon, His response was: "This kind only comes out by prayer" (some Bible translations add "and fasting"). Jesus is clearly implying that earnest prayer (accompanied by fasting?) is a prerequisite for the compelling hand of God to move. I have a godly friend who says, with a twinkle in his eye, "There are only two things in the Bible that are compelled to 'go out' by fasting and prayer—demons and missionaries. And, I prefer to pray for the latter!"[4]

The one part of the instruction that haunts me is the part about praying "earnestly." What does this look like in the life of a church? We need to be more intentional about guiding others to a deeper prayer life for cross-cultural laborers.

> "The compelling hand of God will come upon people in such a way that they will not be able to stay; they will have to go, by their own admission."

Whenever I ask people within a church about the practice of prayer, I always get the response, "Prayer is so important." When I ask how they and their church systematically pray, however, they usually confess that they don't really follow a plan. From my limited exposure to a variety of churches, it appears that prayer is random. Closer examination may reveal that churches have no clear plan for mobilizing prayer for new laborers. In my church, a designated prayer approach is rolled out every other year. Our goal is to get 10 percent of our congregation signed up and praying specifically for new laborers, which is no small task for a church of our size. By signing up, people pledge to pray once a week for two years for new laborers, and they receive updates every two months. A simple prayer guide is made available so everyone can stay focused on praying earnestly (Appendix 4). We have had people as young as eleven and as old as ninety sign up to pray. It is something everyone can do.

## Action Points

1. How can the church increase its opportunities to observe and interact with possible missionary candidates to assess their future potential? What outside resources may help?
2. How can you intentionally integrate an emphasis on praying earnestly for new laborers within your church?

# PART 3

OWNING THE CHURCH'S SPECIAL RELATIONSHIPS

# 7

## THE FUNCTIONAL RELATIONSHIP

The church not only develops a relationship with the missionary; it also grows in its connection with the mission agency. The church is to be the sender of missionaries, and the agency is to be the facilitator. The church has most (but not all) of the resources, and the agency has most (but not all) of the expertise. It makes sense to bring these parties together for productive ministry. It is important to know that "going it alone" often results in the duplication of efforts and a lack of expertise.

When attempting to bring the church and the agency together, it is important to understand their intended roles. An inadequate view of the church's place in missions will diminish its sense of ownership and will create an inaccurate partnership with the agency. "The history of the church in missions has primarily been a history of great personalities or missionary societies. Only in exceptional cases has it been the church in missions. Believers often perceived that missions was the responsibility of individuals rather than the mandate of the church."[1] In his book *A Biblical Theology of Missions*, George Peters called this misperception "[an] unfortunate and abnormal historic development which has produced autonomous, missionless churches on one hand and autonomous churchless missionary societies on the other hand."[2]

Even a casual reading of the New Testament will reveal that the church holds a central position in missions. There are over one hundred references to the church in the New Testament, with a very high percentage of those associated to local congregations. In the book of Acts, we see that the local church became the mediating and authoritative sending body of the New Testament missionary (see Acts 13:1-3). Through further study, apostles of the churches are identified, such as Epaphroditus (see Phil. 2:25) and the "brethren" (see 2 Cor. 8:23, KJV). While Paul and the original twelve were apostles of Jesus Christ, the others became apostles of the churches, receiving their commissioning and authority from the churches. In the classic text of Acts 13, the church leaders in Antioch laid hands on Barnabas and Saul. This speaks to the priority and authority of the local church as the mediating sending agent under the headship of Christ. The practical conclusion is that the church is the sender of missionaries, and today's agency is the facilitator of missionaries. The "Sending Triangle" (Appendix 5) illustrates the important relationship between the church, agency and candidate. Both the church and the agency make significant contributions, but it is important for the church to be seen as the sender. Otherwise, the church will not assume its proper ownership.

Several years ago, an agency introduced an ad campaign that announced, "We have no missionaries; churches have missionaries." This delivered an important message to the Christian public and the church.

---

"Even a casual reading of the New Testament will reveal that the church holds a central position in missions."

---

Many agencies refer to themselves with terms such as "the sending agency" or "sending office." This terminology creates misleading impressions and confusion. Rather, we should speak of it as "the mobilization office" or "agency office." Using "sending" terminology dangerously reinforces an agency's jurisdiction when a church's ecclesiology is weak. To further complicate matters, missionaries are considered employees of their agency. That said, the theological argument takes precedent over any structural argument with the agency world. The sending role is to be reserved for the church, and the agency can assist the church in addressing ministry deficits in the sending effort. Tom Julien says, in his book *Antioch Revisited*, "If missions is what the church does through the missionary and not just for the missionary, that means that the agency must assume more of a servant role toward the church and the church must take more initiative, rather than just remaining passive."[3]

When a local church begins to consider cross-cultural ministry, it often feels inadequate. Many churches have not developed a proven track record overseas. Experience runs very thin. In order to effectively move forward, the church should develop a relationship with an agency or agencies. Just because a church sends monthly support to an agency, it doesn't necessarily have a meaningful relationship with that agency. A good relationship is crucial because the agency has expertise the church may never have. As I mentioned earlier, the church has most of the resources, and the agency has most of the expertise. It makes perfect sense to bring both parties together for productive ministry. Some churches may function without an agency connection, but the vast majority will duplicate ministry efforts if they try to move independently. Churches are sometimes motivated to operate without an agency to avoid a cumbersome process in planning or executing ministry. To resolve this, agencies should develop a flatter organizational approach to decision making rather than a traditional, hierarchical process.

> "Many churches have not developed a proven track record overseas."

Another reason churches abandon agencies is bad previous experiences. A remedy may be to rethink agency relationships altogether, and churches today are becoming more and more intentional in this. Our church has created a preferred agency list. This is a select group of agencies with whom the church desires to cultivate deep working relationships. Narrowing the relational focus has been quite beneficial. We send our candidates to these organizations, we join forces on strategic projects and we regularly invite them into the life of our church. It is important to note that this list is a preferred list, not a required one. However, there are financial incentives in place to strongly encourage our candidates to seek ministry options from the preferred agency list. Every three years we evaluate the list to ensure that we have appropriate participants. It is important to realize that churches either choose their working relationships or inherit them. Numerous churches have spent more time trying to make inherited relationships work than selecting their own preferred partners in ministry.

The relationship between an agency and the church is based on a twofold collaboration foundation. The first part of this foundation is the commitment to each side's indispensable role. Some agencies perceive themselves as being in charge, perhaps due to the indifferent or passive nature of many churches. When it comes to cross-cultural ministry, there are just three types of churches: proactive, reactive or inactive (Appendix 6). Many fall into the reactive category. There are other reasons the agency overshadows the church. It does have most of the knowledge and experience of overseas ministry. In some cases, the agency spends a great deal of time defining their relationship with the receiving church overseas, to the neglect of the sending church.

The second aspect of this collaborative foundation is for each side to be open to being influenced by the other. When influence is allowed in both directions, trust becomes an integral part of the ministry. Some time ago, one of our missionaries found it necessary to return to the United States due to family concerns, an action that fell outside a long-standing policy of the agency. We appealed for flexibility because we believed the policy had outlived its usefulness. After discussion, the agency agreed. This same agency also appealed to us concerning a very different set of circumstances. After gaining a fuller understanding, we determined that their request made sense, and we complied.

In order to ensure this standard of collaborative interchange, the local church should establish certain criteria in selecting a preferred agency partner. The first of these should always be that the agency shares similar vision and values with the church. In other words, both the church and the organization should be moving in the same ministry direction. This, of course, requires the local church to delineate its own ministry vision and values and to take active ownership of them. A very helpful book for churches on this subject is *The Mission Leadership Team* by David Mays, available through www.condeopress.com.

A second criterion is that the agency must provide good field supervision of missionaries. Wrapped up in this expectation is beneficial accountability, a strategic ministry plan for the field and job descriptions for all personnel. The average adult in the North American marketplace is accustomed to these standards and assumes that these practices exist in supported ministries as well. Good agencies can readily provide this for their missionaries and associated churches.

A third criterion is the agency's commitment to quality member care. We have always stated in our church that our greatest resource is our people, and we like to affiliate with agencies that hold a similar view. Does the agency have a member-care office? How do they coordinate member-care efforts with the church? Digressing momentarily, this matter of member care can reveal whether or not an agency views the church as a ministry equal. The level of investment in member care indicates whether or not the agency believes the church is the sender of missionaries. Let me illustrate this. Several years ago, a serious issue was developing in the life of one of our missionaries, and they invited my involvement.

> "When influence is allowed in both directions, trust becomes an integral part of the ministry."

When the situation took a very serious turn, I e-mailed the field several times and asked them to reengage in this unfortunate turn of events. I received no answer. I then e-mailed the agency in an attempt to get some help or an update. When I eventually called, the person who spoke with me explained that, due to privacy laws, they could not even confirm or deny that the person worked for the organization. I asked to speak with a superior and left voice mail messages. After two days, I left a final voice mail stating that if I hadn't received a clarification of what was happening within five business days, I would be forced to discontinue the missionary's monthly support. I received a reply within six hours. I was deeply concerned for our worker. I also was surprised and distressed that the sending church was viewed as an unnecessary part of this member-care process. The lack of response was due to a complete breakdown of member-care protocol on the field. The agency had been irresponsible, and this neglect cost us a worker.

The good that resulted from this painful situation was the formulation of a process. Now, all of our missionaries are required to sign a release of information form. It identifies two people within the church and two people in the agency who can always share information about the worker without breaking confidentiality. An attorney has reviewed this agreement, and the form is available in Appendix 7.

A fourth key criterion is for agencies to treat churches as equal partners. I serve within a large church ministry; but agencies should respect churches, regardless of their size. Churches should question whether the agency appears to value the church's contributions and input.

Finally, the fifth of these criteria is that the agency should demonstrate fiscal responsibility. Is the administrative fee deducted from monthly support a reasonable amount? Can the organization provide a specific itemization of a worker's monthly support structure? Does the organization end in the black each year? Is there a sense of financial integrity? A document from Catalyst Services entitled "Measuring Agency Partnership Potential" (Appendix 8) flags ten collaboration indicators that churches can look for in agencies. I deeply appreciate what George Miley says in his book *Loving the Church . . . Blessing the Nations: Pursuing the Role of Local Churches in Global Mission*; he affirms that learning to relate to each other in a godly way is not just a structural issue—it is also a character issue.[4] Certainly, we must all realize that there is no perfect church or agency. We will always need to lead with grace and kindness, relating to others in the same way that we want to be treated.

## Relational Touchpoints

The church and the agency do well to discuss some relational touchpoints as they collaborate, providing an opportunity to forge a mutually supportive friendship. When people declare their interest and availability for cross-cultural ministry, their call needs to be affirmed. This is our first touchpoint. It is critical for a church to affirm a person's potential and readiness, even if the church does not feel suited to do so. In some situations, the church may form an opinion on a person's call and ask an agency for a second opinion. If a church has reservations about an individual, it may be opportune for an agency to offer an assessment, since it may be more objective. This can be a teachable moment for everyone involved. When the agency is invited into a process, it is important that it equips rather than replaces the church. The agency can use this request for help to develop a meaningful friendship. Anytime a candidate observes the participation of the church and the agency in their personal progression, it becomes a significant learning opportunity, and everyone experiences collaborative ministry.

> "Certainly, we must all realize that there is
> no perfect church or agency."

A second relational touchpoint to develop is ministry vision. If a church has a developed vision and plans to execute that vision, then the agency can serve these ministry aspirations. If this overlaps with initiatives of the agency, there may be real potential to network and use creativity for shared ministry. If a church struggles to develop vision for ministry, then the agency can come alongside to discuss opportunities and to guide the church in an exploratory process. Some churches may benefit from established, ongoing field ministries. Originating something completely new may energize others. The involvement of field leadership and their sending churches, along with other interested churches, can lead to ministry expansion. Placing our dreams and inclinations in front of one another creates traction for cooperative ministry.

Another critical touchpoint for all parties is collaborative decision making on shared personnel. Churches active in the missions arena view their missionaries as a resource of the church, as does the agency. There should never be any "act and inform" on the part of the missionary, the sending church or the agency. If unilateral decisions are made, then it is not a healthy partnership model. The most pivotal issue to consider is: Who steers the missions agenda of the church? If undue influence or decision making comes from outside the church, then those inside the church will become frustrated with ministry that is no longer under their supervision. Because of this scenario, local churches have had to develop procedures to avoid unsolicited outside influence. While in a previous church ministry, we faced a situation in which an agency indirectly informed us that our missionary would have to move into a different role and ministry because it had a placement gap to fill. This was very frustrating for our missionary, as he was not equipped for the alternative function and would have to leave a ministry that was finally beginning to bear fruit and that might face irrecoverable setbacks if he left. In this instance, missions leadership in the church stepped forward and advocated for the missionary and his work, and they clarified the church's view of partnership to the agency. This incident of unilateral decision making was the impetus for developing a document to include in my master's project entitled "Right of Review."

> Because we view ourselves as partners in ministry with our missionaries, our church reserves the right to review and respond at any point in time to partnership changes. What this means is that if any change in the missionary's status occurs (whether it

be a change in location, ministry activity, theology or philosophy of ministry, regardless of whether it is a change prompted by the desire of the missionary or their agency) our church and its missions committee reserves the right of review to (if deemed appropriate) alter the financial support commitment of the church to that missionary. It is recognized and understood that a missionary may well be pursing the will of God in service in an area that is not necessarily the will of God for our church to support. For this reason it is vital that the missions committee of the church be notified promptly when such changes are being considered so the review process can be handled in a proper and expeditious manner.[5]

This policy has served the purpose of generating good communication among the sending church, the missionary and the agency. The agency should not be expected to discuss major issues with all the missionary's supporters; this is reserved for the sending church. Other major supporters can always be included in communications at the missionary's discretion.

One additional touchpoint is member care of missionaries. It is best for all parties to share their expectations regarding member care. If any issue consistently disrupts a missionary's ministry effectiveness, family well-being or personal integrity, discussions should occur with the missionary, the church and the agency. Shared time, expertise, concern and funding can provide an effective restorative process for those in need. In ministry cooperation, we have occasionally brought people back to the United States and arranged what we call a rest and renewal plan. Member care issues and action are disclosed only to those in leadership roles within select ministries.

> "We will always need to lead with grace and kindness, relating to others in the same way that we want to be treated."

These are just a few touchpoints that should be discussed by all participants. As ministry continues, additional touchpoints will become necessary. For instance, across the North American church there is a movement to send out church-based, church-planting teams. There may be up to a dozen adults from the same church on the team. Because a large number of workers are coming from one sending church, that church will desire to engage in ministry at a fairly high level. This may already be our next touchpoint. In the days ahead there will be many new challenges and opportunities. It will be most rewarding to face them together.

## Why an Agency?

Working together generates friendships, ideas, resources and opportunities for everyone. Several years ago, I attended a "Drive" conference featuring Andy Stanley and his church ministry in Atlanta. One of the messages of the conference was "Partner; Don't Pioneer." There is great wisdom in this. We should use the connection points that are already available to us. Supervising missionaries at great distances in incredibly different cultures and political climates is unlike anything else the local church does. We cannot disregard the long hours and considerable efforts that go into bookkeeping, health insurance, immigration issues, emergency evacuation procedures, child education options and effectively contextualized ministry. In *Here to There*, David Meade points out, "Local churches tend to overstate their abilities and underestimate the complexities of functioning as their own mission agency."[6] No one is suggesting that collaboration is easy—but it is worthwhile.

## Action Points

1. Visit or revisit the need for affirming your vision and values. Is your outlook up-to-date? Can leaders succinctly communicate your vision?
2. If there is no unified vision for cross-cultural ministry, identify some steps to get there. Who will be responsible for developing the vision? What are your resources to get the job done? What is the timeline for completion?
3. Come to some conclusions about how you can establish or improve your church and agency relationships.
4. How can the agency help the local church be what it was intended to be? How can the local church help the agency be what it was intended to be?

# 8

# THE STRATEGIC RELATIONSHIP
## WHAT ARE THE REMAINING UNFINISHED TASKS?

Jesus Christ has commissioned the church to make disciples of all nations. To complete this commission, the local church must know what task remains to be finished. It is easy to set any ministry on autopilot rather than to think and act strategically. In order to complete the task, the church must strategically utilize its resources. We have to ask ourselves, "If every church missions program looked exactly like ours, would the Great Commission ever be completed?"

Missions should be less about going to places and more about going to people.

Just as you and I have many opportunities to build special relationships, so too does the local church. While we may be able to manage a number of relationships, we still need to decide which ones are the most important and invest in them. When Jesus Christ talked to His followers on the evening of resurrection day, He mentioned their future relationship to the world. He emphasized this important relationship throughout the following forty days. Moments before returning to heaven, He instructed them one final time. They were to make disciples among every tribe, language, people and nation. These followers, and all others to come, were to go throughout all the world to do this. They were to make these disciples both locally and globally. This should be the strategic relationship for every local church. Every local expression of Christ followers should prioritize this commission with their time and attention. Jesus Christ told His disciples, "My food is to do the will of him who sent me and to accomplish his work" (John 4:34). Christ died that He, the just, might bring us, the unjust, to God (see 1 Pet. 3:18).

---

"Every local expression of Christ followers should prioritize this commission with their time and attention."

---

He fully intended for His followers to accomplish the mission given them as well. He longs to build a new, redeemed and united community among all peoples. In order to accomplish this assignment, today's local church needs to think strategically.

The first step in thinking strategically is being fully informed about what the Head of the church is calling local churches to do. The charge is to make disciples of all nations. The second step is learning what work has been done and what work remains. Agencies should assist the church in securing some of this information. The church needs this information in order to more meaningfully contribute to the remaining unfinished task. Ministry effort should be more calculated and less redundant. In his book *Missions: Biblical Foundations and Contemporary Strategies*, Gailyn Van Rheenen offers helpful insights into strategic thinking. His discussion centers primarily on strategies for ministry contexts outside North America, but he provides an important philosophy of strategy. He claims it is not enough for Christians to be busy. "Christian strategists who prioritize God's role in missions do not begin with the pragmatic question 'Does it work?'"[1] The question instead should be, "Does it fit my theology?" It is important for the local church and its decision-making process to mirror the desires, perspective and nature of God.

A church needs to know if something is applicable to the remaining unfinished task, so it is also useful to define strategic tasks. A basic working definition of the term *strategic* in this specific context is 'meeting a critical need while magnifying important influence to build the church where it is weak or nonexistent.' Each met need should be related to the greater unfinished task. The influence resulting from meeting the need should be catalytic for the building of the church. When churches start thinking strategically, they realize how reactive they have been. Being strategic is about being proactive and intentional. Being strategic is about establishing correct priorities and building ministry plans that pursue those priorities.

Thinking and planning strategically better equips the church to perceive which needs are critical. Having a defined plan also keeps audiences clear and informed on why the church is focusing on certain opportunities.

> "Ministry effort should be more calculated and less redundant."

I remember someone coming up to me after a church service once to remind me that there are lost people all around us and our church. He was reacting to our emphasis to go to the least reached. He failed to understand, however, that being strategic has less to do with one's spiritual condition and more to do with access to the gospel. It was commendable that he was concerned about the lost, but he had not yet realized it was partially his responsibility to reach the lost around him. Believers in the United States don't need to financially support someone in their community to make disciples when they themselves are gospel carriers. Whenever a people group develops a viable, indigenous community of believing Christ followers with adequate numbers and resources to evangelize without outside assistance, the people around them are considered reached. "This is not to say that there is no work to do among them. There most certainly is! It is to say that the primary agent for doing the work is now in place. It is Christ himself, present in his churches to the extent where the churches are able to minister to their own culture."[2] At this point, the "agent" in place should be the community of believers in that area and not the missionary.

It may be useful here to differentiate between the terms *evangelism* and *missions*. *Evangelism* is reaching people who don't believe in Jesus. *Missions* is reaching people who don't know there is a Jesus to believe in. George Murray often addresses this issue in his extensive travels to speak to churches about missions:

> Are there people in the world who still don't know there is a Jesus to believe in? Absolutely. Based on highly sophisticated and accurate research, it is estimated that there are over two billion people living today who are in that category. Many of these people have never met a Christian. Many of these people have never seen a church building. For them, the Bible is an unknown book, and the cross is an unknown symbol. For many of them, Christmas and Easter are not in their calendar. While we wait with joyful anticipation for Christ's Second Coming, these people have never heard of His First Coming. These people live on the other side of the border of gospel availability. Not only have they never heard the gospel message from a flesh and blood Christian, but most of these people have no radio, cell phone, or computer access to the gospel message. Many are illiterate. These people are not only lost (don't believe in Jesus), but they are unreached (don't know there is a Jesus to believe in). In many cases they are out of reach and won't be reached unless someone from the outside deliberately penetrates their people group or culture. These people need missionaries. These are the kind of people to whom missionaries go.[3]

As my church's Global Ministries pastor, I have entered into discussions on whether or not the heathen are lost. This discussion concerns the eternal destiny of people who die without ever having received an understandable explanation of the gospel. Scripture indicates that people bear personal responsibility for their lost condition (see Ps. 19:1–4; Rom. 1:19–20; 2:14–16). Many people cannot accept the uncomfortable reality that the heathen are lost. At some point in the conversation, I interject that perhaps this awkward discussion is less a reflection on God and more a reflection on the church. God has done everything necessary to provide a plan of redemption for this needy world. Can we say the same about the church? The church has spent two millenniums doing less important things, yet we absolve ourselves of this tragedy rather quickly and point the finger at God. We need to take a good look at our local church and ask ourselves the question, "Has our church done everything necessary to share the plan of redemption with a needy world?"

Approximately two thousand years have passed since the Great Commission was given. This commission calls us to make disciples among all ethnic groups and all nations (see Matt. 28:18–20). A lot has been done, but much remains to be done. It is not enough to evangelize. Those who come to faith are to be discipled; they are to be brought to faith and obedience in Jesus Christ.

Local and global ministry efforts should enable the continuation of the Great Commission. I remember a helpful illustration that came out of an Urbana[4] conference years ago. The image was of a group of people holding a heavy log. On one end of the log were six or seven people, and at the other end of the log was one person struggling to hold up that end. The caption underneath was, "Where is the critical need?" This illustration asked its viewers to consider the weight of the unfinished task and to examine where there is a need for more workers. Strategic thinking assists churches as they commit themselves and their resources to reaching the unreached.

> "Has our church done everything necessary to share the plan of redemption with a needy world?"

Once we recognize that our task is to make disciples of all the nations, or people groups, of the world, the logical next step is to figure out what part of that task is unaddressed. Whenever we talk about people not yet engaged with the gospel, we always run the risk of forgetting a very important group. We could focus on the 10/40 Window as a region of the world that lacks the benefit of being able to hear the gospel. This, however, can be disheartening to those who are focusing on the spiritual darkness of Europe. There are pockets of people groups in every region of the world without a gospel witness. My advice is for each church to do some of its own research. The website Joshuaproject.net is useful for getting acquainted with the people groups of the world. To illustrate the remaining need, let's consider the 10/40 Window. This window is an imaginary window between the tenth latitude and the fortieth latitude on a globe. A high percentage of unreached people groups are in this window. It represents gospel-resistant blocks of Muslims, Hindus and Buddhists. It also represents the largest number of poor in our world. Some of these people are in restricted-access countries. There is limited religious freedom for people in these countries. There are acute physical and spiritual needs. If every Christian in this region of the world were to witness to every neighbor in his or her community, the vast majority of peoples would still not have any opportunity to hear the good news. This poses a challenge to the body of Christ: What percentage of funds or personnel from your church are engaging people in this window with the gospel? Examine your revenue and your support figures. How is your church strategically using the resources God has given you?

> "There are pockets of people groups in every region of the world without a gospel witness."

In *A Practical Theology of Missions*, Eric Wright quotes an article by Mark Orr that shared the findings of well-known researcher David Barrett: "In our 'global village' world there are 285,000 active cross-cultural Christian missionaries. . . . Amazingly, about 91 percent of the missionaries work with and around Christians; about 8 percent work with evangelized non-Christians; and 1 percent, or just under 3,000 missionaries, work with the unevangelized."[5] There needs to be a careful evaluation of missionary placement. This is a discussion for both the church and the agency. It is no longer enough for the field leadership of agencies to simply state the need for more workers. A stronger rationale is needed that includes a longer-term plan and careful, national church input whenever possible. Churches will need to ask more direct questions about placement, and agencies should be ready with missiological and practical reasons for any placement.

Facilitators are needed to help missionaries reach the unreached, as illustrated by George Murray's interaction with a missionary pilot:

> I still get emotional when I recall a meaningful missionary aviation flight I had in a small plane over the rainforests of Irian Jaya (now Papua) in eastern Indonesia. Since the flight was going to be over two hours long, the missionary pilot put the plane on autopilot in order to pull out and show me a large chart of the territory over which we were flying. On that chart he had marked fourteen locations where there were still totally unreached tribal groups, people who were still waiting to hear the gospel for the first time. With tears in his eyes, he told me about his constant prayer that all fourteen of those tribal groups would soon be able to hear the gospel, and he told me with excitement how he couldn't wait to see airstrips built and gospel-preaching missionaries flown into all of those unreached areas. Yes, that pilot was passionate about flying, but he saw his role as a means to the end of preaching the gospel and planting the Church among unreached people. Amen![6]

One additional issue to briefly reflect on when considering the remaining unfinished task is the gospel-resistant areas of the world. "Prospective missionary candidates are often urged to 'Go where the action is.' Such an appeal resonates with our natural instincts, brought up as we are to be familiar with marketing strategy. Why knock your head against a brick wall ministering where it is hard and few people are converted, when accepted missionary theory allows you to go where there are results?"[7] This is a real issue for the church and the agency, especially when the focus is on finishing the task. It may prove helpful for churches and agencies to collaborate on developing a position paper on such a matter. It is important for everyone to remember that the Great Commission calls us to go into *all* the world (see Mark 16:15). It specifically states that we are to make disciples of *all* nations (see Matt. 28:19–20). Taking up this call means going into gospel-resistant zones. There is something special and honorable about those who are serving by sowing, planting or watering the gospel seed in hard areas. Some plant, others water, but God gives the increase. Each will receive his wages according to his labor (see 1 Cor. 3:6–8). In most cases, the harvesting of today represents the hard work of soil preparation and abundant sowing. This is a God-appointed ministry; where would we be without sowers?

Today's hard places will be the harvesting fields of tomorrow as we sow. Many Bible characters ministered for long periods of time with little immediate effect, and I myself have seen ministry timelines that are thirty years long. Only in the last half decade has the more exciting harvest come. Who relishes the thought of persevering for long periods of time? The North American church is especially impatient in this area. We can learn much from the body of Christ in the hard places. There is a need to apply ourselves to preparing for a harvest. This kind of effort is vital to completing the task.

> "It is important for everyone to remember that the Great Commission calls us to go into *all* the world."

Finally, I want to point out that God has people on the move. In light of what we are called to do, George Murray illustrates the changes in our world that cause us to realize that missions should be less about going to places (geographical) and more about going to peoples (sociological).

> Because of the huge migration of the world's peoples today, it is becoming increasingly difficult to identify specific geographic areas of the world as "mission fields". While it is certainly not wrong to say that places like North Africa, or Central Asia, or the Middle East, or India, or Tibet (to name just a few areas) are "mission fields," in seeking to reach the least-reached peoples on earth, we might do well to identify the unreached ethnically or demographically rather than geographically. So, a strategy to reach the unreached Hindu Sikhs might concentrate its efforts in north India and in western Canada, where there is a critical mass of Sikhs who have migrated from India (and who, in some cases, are more open to the gospel message than they were back in their mother country and culture). Or, a strategy to reach the largely unreached Kurds of northern Iraq and southern Turkey might also concentrate

its missionary efforts on Houston Texas where there is a significantly large Kurdish refugee camp. My understanding is that a local Southern Baptist Church in Houston has reached out to the Kurdish refugee population in their city. A local church of Kurdish believers has now been planted near Houston and believers in that new church are traveling back to northern Iraq and southern Turkey to share the gospel with their families there. A missionary strategy to reach North African Muslims might include an outreach to the millions of North African Muslims who have now immigrated to Western Europe. All of the above is effective missionary work, not because of where it is located, but because it is concentrating on reaching otherwise unreached people.

We see pictures of refugees. Many of us have been introduced to international students. People from limited-access regions of the world are coming to us. This has implications for the church if we take our strategic relationship to the remaining unfinished task seriously.

There is something special and honorable about those who are serving by sowing, planting, or watering the gospel seed in hard areas.

Within a twenty-mile radius of our church, more than forty different languages are spoken. In our church's facilities, we offer weekly ministry in Spanish, Russian, Mandarin and Arabic. I was recently told that there are approximately two thousand Arabic speakers in our community. Our sought-after audiences are coming to us! There are special ministries in the New York metropolitan area for the unreached who come to the city. The attempt is to reach some and help them catch a vision for reaching their own people in their country of origin. This is happening everywhere. Every church should educate themselves about their changing communities. Ministry to the unreached may be just a few miles away.

## Action Points

1. What are the key definitions of the missions emphasis in your church? Where might you need to clarify helpful definitions and distinctions?

2. As you begin to assess the present state of your missions efforts, what percentage of missionaries and money go to the 10/40 Window? What are you learning as you assess?

3. What cross-cultural ministry potential might you have within a reasonable radius of your church? Who in your community can do research to help the church make informed decisions about local cross-cultural ministry?

# PART 4

## OWNING THE CHURCH'S SPECIAL CHALLENGES

# 9

# THE DANGER IN BECOMING
# A SENDING-CHURCH MODEL

There are real challenges to becoming an effective sending church. This chapter deals with the subtle shift in focus that results in time, attention and resources being given to the messengers at the expense of the mandate. When we bond with missionaries, we also need to bond with their passion for the people they seek to reach. We must love the unreached as we love the sent. When we confuse the means with the end, we lose our strategic edge. How do we design our ministry to emphasize both the worker and the work? This chapter will lay out a game plan for developing a healthy balance.

When a church becomes a sending church, ministry becomes more personal. As people who have been integral to the life of the church serve overseas, relational and emotional bonds are stretched halfway around the world. Within our church, we have often asserted that while relationships with missionaries change, they do not end. Why then would I write a chapter on the danger of becoming a sending church? Since this ministry is very relational, a great deal of time and effort is spent shepherding people to whom churches are committed. It is easy to get caught up in the volume of details that require daily or weekly attention, but it is vital for church leadership to catch the macro picture of what God is doing through the missions-sending ministry. It is exciting to pause for macro reflection and to realize that God is not done writing this story.

---

"We must love the unreached as we love the sent."

---

More than eight years ago, I set aside two complete days in December to engage in some long-term planning. I attempt to do this each year in December because it is the slowest month of the year for missions. I spent one full day poring over missionary retirement projections for the next ten years. I discovered that almost 30 percent of our missionaries were going to move into retirement over a rapidly approaching seven-year time frame. This had implications for the entire ministry. Would we develop a new, energized approach to recruit new workers to replace those who were retiring? How would we redirect monthly support? How would we care for and utilize our retired field workers in home ministry? I gave recommendations to our church's elders in the form of a report.

The greatest macro realization, however, came to me earlier in my ministry. It was quite a surprise. Between 1991 and 1996, I worked to complete a master's degree. As is often the case, I was required to complete a research project before graduation, and I addressed the topic of developing and implementing a philosophy of missions in the local church. The project consumed about eighteen months, and it impacted my life and ministry more than I ever anticipated. One significant source I referenced was the May–June 1995 *Mission Frontiers* bulletin of the U.S. Center for World Mission (now known as Frontier Ventures). This issue provided a series of articles entitled, "Is Some Missions Work More Important than Others?" This material stretched my ministry paradigm. The next issue of the magazine had an article called, "Adopt-A-People: A way to love missionaries and the people they work with," by Stan Yoder that revealed the real danger of the sending-church model. The article reviewed the experience of a missionary couple and how their ministry focus differed from that of their supporting churches. They had been missionaries to the Yalunka people of Sierra Leone, West Africa, and had returned to the United States for health reasons after ten years of service. They attempted to visit and update their supporting churches on these developments. This was their experience:

> I asked our missions committee members if any were still praying for the Yalunkas. Their reply was no, we are praying for your family and your ministry in Pasadena. Our church had us, and not the Yalunkas. Yet

the Yalunkas are the ones in desperate need of prayer for release from Islam and animism. We went to this tribal group to bring men and women to Jesus. Our goal was to see a church-planting movement started so that all Yalunkas would have the opportunity to know God and give Him the glory He deserves. Yet I'm afraid our supporters did not fully share in this goal with us. Why? They had a different focus.[1]

What was this different focus? There are numerous churches that adopt the worker but not the work. Missions activity in sending and supporting churches is often related to those with whom they have a relationship—the missionaries. They have invested their resources and emotions in them. It's important to remember, however, that missionaries are sent to lost, unreached people, and these people are the ones in need of support. Unfortunately, sometimes churches direct time, attention and resources to the messengers at the expense of the mandate. In many ministries, going overseas can appear to be the ultimate expression of any missions commitment, which makes the process of sending an end in itself. The goal of the local church, however, is to help reach the unreached, to complete the remaining unfinished task. The purpose is not simply to send missionaries. Although it's never the intention of people or churches to develop an exclusive focus on the worker, this easily happens. We are naturally drawn to missionaries as people we know; sometimes they even grew up in our church. We admire their willingness to leave the familiar and go into the world. While we bond with these missionaries, we need to also bond with their passion for the people they seek to reach. We must love the unreached as we love the sent. When we confuse the means with the end, we lose our strategic edge.

It is often the case that when missionaries transition back to the United States, their ministry vision returns with them. It is the exception for churches or individuals to sustain an overseas focus in the absence of missionaries. The sending model is most vulnerable to the missionaries' vision being transitory and returning stateside with them. In his book *Antioch Revisited*, Tom Julien states, "Missions is not what the church does for the missionary but what the church does through the missionary."[2] I would add that it is what the church does through and with the missionary. Julien says further, "It would be a new way of looking at the missionary—seeing him or her as the vital link between the church and the nations of the world and as an indispensable element for fulfilling the church's mission through teamwork. The missionary would not merely be someone who comes occasionally to share about his work in order to gain financial support."[3]

---

"Sending must be maintained as a means to an end rather than an end in itself."

---

When we see the missionary fulfilling the church's mission through teamwork with the sending church, there is a more complete ownership of the vision. Churches should undergird missionaries' ministries as well as send them. Sending must be maintained as a means to an end rather than an end in itself. Our supreme motivation is the completion of the Great Commission.

Here is the critical question: How can we adopt both the worker and the work? Both the worker and the work must be appropriately highlighted in our ministries. The church and the agency must work together to lead the way forward. We can probe more deeply into this topic by beginning with some simple steps.

---

> "Both the worker and the work must be appropriately highlighted in our ministries."

---

The very first effort in adopting both the worker and the work should be to develop an intentional focus on the remaining unfinished task. Ministry investors need to know the endgame. In the church where I serve, we drafted a position paper on the least reached (Appendix 9). This is a document used in missions education around the church, and it acts as a standard for accountability. This focus is to be integrated into the complete life of the church. Candidates in our church-based missionary preparation course get acquainted with this position and its implications regarding worker deployment. Children and youth hear about the least reached. Adults are introduced to unreached people groups through the Joshua Project and Google Earth. The material is found in our training literature. Agencies should include a focus on the remaining unfinished task in a vision or mission statement and communicate it with missionary candidates prior to any orientation session. The remaining task should be represented in mobilization tools that focus on a variety of audiences.

We need to develop advocates for the worker and the work. Churches and organizations should discuss four penetrating questions to evaluate their relationship with the work. These questions shed light on global ministry commitments and action.

## 1. The Question of Evaluation

Evaluate your present ministry model.

Q: If every local church modeled its global ministry efforts after the global ministry efforts of your church or agency, would the Great Commission be completed? Why or why not?

What did this question reveal regarding ministry strengths and weaknesses?

## 2. The Question of Completion

Evaluate your present relationship to remaining unfinished tasks in the Great Commission.

Global context: Presently, there are more than two billion people outside the reach of the gospel (i.e., they live where it is highly unlikely or impossible for them to hear the gospel in their lifetime). To share the gospel with them, some believers must cross barriers of distance, language and culture.

Q: How would you describe your church's or agency's relationship to the remaining unfinished task?

Circle one:

Nonexistent | Weak | Average

Expanding | Healthy

What should shape the future of this relationship?

## 3. The Question of Acceleration

Evaluate your present level of motivation and urgency to make disciples of all nations.

Biblical context: We believe that Jesus Christ alone is the way, the truth and the life. Millions perish outside of Christ each year and are lost for eternity.

Q: What evidence of a Christ-honoring motivation to bring the gospel to those in need is there in your church or agency?

What should be the source of your motivation, and how can it be properly expressed?

## 4. The Question of Incursion

Evaluate your willingness to be intentional in pursuing Christ's command to make disciples of all nations.

Biblical context: Jesus Christ declares in Matthew 16:18 that He will build His church, and He states that the gates of hell will not prevail against it. The picture He gives is of the church threatening the very gates of hell. The church only becomes a threat when it proactively moves forward.

Q: In what ways is your church or agency on the offensive in global ministry?

Is your church's or agency's posture in cross-cultural ministry best described as inactive, reactive or proactive? (See Appendix 10 for a description of different traits of an inactive, reactive and proactive church.) Note the specific characteristics that lead to your conclusion about your church.

The second effort in adopting both the worker and the work is to secure the assistance of other recognized leaders. Many church workers and missionaries have their focus on the right things, but they may find it difficult to share their audience with other initiatives, especially when each ministry is equally passionate about their goals. Developing balance among individual messages takes time and patience and must be grounded in a level of godly character. In securing the help of others, it is essential to convey the reason for equally emphasizing the worker and the work. It is imperative to nurture leadership that understands and embraces this emphasis.

The third effort is to introduce global narrative, telling stories of spiritual need and of life change so the audience can see the people who are being reached as more than just numbers or abstract concepts. The audience within the local church should be able to recall mental images of their missionaries and their ministry relationships. Visuals of unengaged or newly engaged people can be displayed in the form of art, while names and faces should become a part of prayer times. Presenting the ministry context in story form to others allows it to become personal and therefore unforgettable. This should drive the use of communication in its various forms. (Caution is needed, however, when using social media in cases of ministry among the least reached or areas particularly hostile to the gospel.)

The fourth effort is to cultivate a balance of priority in ministry, giving attention to both the worker and the work. This can come from leadership, the pulpit and the workers themselves. The size of a church may determine the possibility for missionaries to participate in church services. Be creative in finding or inventing new venues for the dual emphasis. Leverage the church's calendar of events and unique opportunities to introduce both concepts. Missions education is an especially appropriate time to discuss the endgame and the means to that end. This sort of instruction should appear on the church calendar.

> "Developing balance among individual messages takes time and patience and must be grounded in a level of godly character."

The fifth effort is to make connections to nationals. This can be done through the use of media or through personal visits to their location or vice versa. Meeting those who have been impacted by a ministry can be a powerful experience. The body of Christ can greatly benefit from hearing testimonies from people around the world who have been transformed by the gospel message. Thoughtful communication reminds us why we do what we do.

The final effort centers on focusing on the spiritually needy places of our world where there are so few workers. Over ten years ago, our church's global ministry scoped out the country of Cambodia, where we had no workers serving. We wanted to learn what it would take to reach the poor and marginalized people of this country. Through a partnership formed with five other churches in the United States and a relief and development organization, we joined this ministry and learned a great deal. We sent numerous short-termers to Cambodia, we prayed for the country and we threw ourselves into this initiative. The Lord taught us many valuable lessons. Our involvement in Cambodia continues to be a healthy experience for us as a church. Today, we have two missionary families serving in Cambodia as a result of our basic ministry efforts. We have had several Cambodians visit our church and minister to us. All this came because we knew we needed to be stretched in a new way to emphasize the worker and the work. Now we are introducing the country of Malawi to our congregation. This is another totally new experience for us. We presently have no missionaries in this country. Our Lord instructed His disciples to lift up their eyes and see that the fields are white for harvest (see John 4:35). This is what will help mobilize the church of today; we can help make disciples among all nations as we adopt the worker and the work.

## Action Points

1. Consider your own church's history. What do you see as a blessing? A challenge? A potential danger? Why?
2. Is there evidence that your church has adopted the worker but not the work? What is the evidence? What would an outside observer say is your cross-cultural endgame? Why?
3. Which of the four penetrating questions should be discussed first by your missions leadership? Why? Which should be discussed second? Why?
4. What organizations or resources would help your ministry move forward? What plan can you set in place to contact or access them?

# 10

# THE DANGER OF DISTRACTIONS
## WHAT KEEPS THE CHURCH FROM BEING
## EFFECTIVE SENDERS?

Mission creep and mission drift are two distractions that receive little attention but that must be addressed. Mission creep occurs when objectives are expanded well beyond original goals. It dilutes the original purpose and broadens efforts, which results in a loss of priorities. Mission drift involves wandering from the original purpose and eventually replacing that purpose. While the means to an end may well change, the endgame should never change. These distractions, among other corporate and individual struggles, can derail effective ministry.

Examine the North American church's commitment to missions and you will see a mandate that has fallen into neglect. It is true that a number of churches do press forward in applying the Great Commission to their ministry plans and resources. Yet the motivation of the majority of churches has diminished, and churches' focus on making disciples of all nations has weakened. Denominations document the shrinking percentage of money given to missions. Comparing the percentage of giving to missions to domestic spending typically reveals that we spend a disproportionate sum of money on ourselves. There are many things that distract individuals and churches away from the Great Commission; and if terms aren't defined, it's possible to justify nearly any investment as missions spending.

> "Mission drift involves wandering from the original purpose and eventually replacing that purpose."

According to Wikipedia, mission creep is "the expansion of a project or mission beyond its original goals, often after initial successes." Michael Horton is concerned that churches are being distracted by mission creep. He explains this concern by referring to an article written by Jim Hoagland: "The term was originally coined in a 1993 *Washington Post* article on the UN Peacekeeping mission in Somalia, in which the writer argued that a humanitarian mission turned into a military operation which did not have clearly spelled-out goals and for which the soldiers on the ground were not prepared."[1] Missions means different things to different people. To one person, missions can mean baking a pie and giving it to a new neighbor. There is nothing inappropriate about doing this Christian act of kindness and love. But applying the term "missions" to it broadens its meaning until it loses the distinctions that give us focus and purpose. At Calvary Church, we now use the title "Global Ministries" for our missions ministry and define it as "crossing barriers of distance, language and culture to make disciples among all nations for the glory of God." We clearly defined our terms and parameters to ensure our understanding and practice of missions did not become diluted. In the absence of definition, "missions" may become something very different from what God intended.

The church's sometimes weak views on its commission are rooted in inadequate explanations of Jesus' commission, as well as in cultural influences that pull church members in myriad directions, causing us to lose sight of our true purpose. The first issue to tackle is the lack of understanding about the Great Commission and how churches can effectively practice it. The Great Commission charges the church with the responsibility of making disciples of all nations or people groups. Since all nations are involved, the immediate application for churches is to somehow become global. Any size church can pray and join forces with others in partnership toward more influential and effective overseas ministry. Any church can give and cooperate with other churches or organizations to send short-term teams. Any church's membership can tithe toward some type of ministry to the nations. Any church can get in the game both locally and cross-culturally.

However, many churches do not take any of these basic steps. One reason for this is that few models exist of churches practicing global ministry efforts. Although large churches sponsor an abundance of conferences across the country that meet real and specific needs, churches still have no readily available network for global ministry development. In his book *When Missions Shapes the Mission: You and Your Church Can Reach the World*, David Horner states that 90 percent of the ministry models to which pastors in his denomination are exposed have not demonstrated even a functional commitment to missions.[2] What leaders or pastors know and experience becomes normative. It is easy for us to become satisfied with what has always been done, especially when we look around and see so many churches doing less. Churches need to find healthy ministry role models that challenge them to grow in their faith and commitment to missions. Many churches that have practiced missions over the years are becoming less effective and influential. There are reasons for this. One reason worth discussing is defined in *Mission Drift: The Unspoken Crisis Facing Leaders, Charities, and Churches*. In this book, Peter Greer and Chris Horst point out that many churches are dangerously drifting from their organization's original purpose. Many churches begin well with missions but don't effectively maintain their focus.

"Missions means different things to different people."

The question is: What will it take for a church to continue well or end well? *Mission Drift*, an excellent resource for any ministry, lists three things about mission-true organizations. Each organization needs to understand their reason for existing, what is immutable and what can change. They must understand that the endgame never changes but that the means to that end may well change. Finally, they should not stagnate but should embrace change when it helps them stay effective in accomplishing their purpose.[3]

The end does not, of course, justify any means. I am just asserting that we never should confuse the means with the end. Churches are often guilty of remaining loyal and protective of means that have outlived their usefulness. Change must be introduced carefully and thoughtfully. Change should only be embraced when it helps the church, missionary and agency stay effective in accomplishing their purpose. That said, there are many things that do change over time. Doors to ministry open and close. Political activity and needs of the world and the church fluctuate dramatically. Our ministry context for global ministry changes constantly. Only a few basic things must never change. Each church should determine what these things are with their pastors, elders and other appropriate ministry authorities.

Every day as I go to work at Calvary Church, I think about our missions legacy, and I feel the weight of responsibility to leave the ministry in a better condition than when I joined it. If your church does not yet have such a legacy, you should realize that God has you where you are to build one that will honor and please Him. Building and/or sustaining an effective cross-cultural ministry does not happen by accident. We all need to be effective stewards of the ministries God has entrusted to us.

---

"Churches need to find healthy ministry role models that challenge them to grow in their faith and commitment to missions."

---

Missions work has died in churches that were once known to be great senders. This happens for multiple reasons. In many cases there was never any succession plan to turn missions responsibilities over to the next generation. Missions may have been so dear to the heart of one or two people in the church that they would not entrust it to anyone else; they did not have the foresight or ability to train others in the next generation to advance missions. When the "missions people" die or move, missions growth dies as well. How then can a legacy for missions be developed and sustained in a church? First, it is very important for the church to have a clear missions statement regarding its vision and values. Second, it is critical to carefully and prayerfully recruit participants before an urgent need exists. These contributors can be either hired staff or volunteers. Every church needs to discuss how it will keep missions central to the life of the church, and to determine what can grow and transform and what should never change. Casting a compelling vision for missions is necessary for ensuring its future.

A second distraction for the church is the temptation to use resources for its own programs. The Western church has more resources than we realize, and we sometimes fail to maintain a correct perspective concerning those resources. A piece of this incorrect mind-set was revealed to George Murray in a conversation he had after speaking at an annual missions conference.

Once I was speaking in a church at their annual missions conference, and I gave a strong message on the need for more people to leave their families, friends, country and church to go to the unreached mission fields of the world. An older gentleman in that congregation took issue with my strong emphasis on the need for people to "leave home and go," so he sought me out at the end of that event and gave me a mild but firm tongue-lashing. "Young man," he said to me in a resistant tone, "don't forget that in war time, for every one soldier who goes to the front lines, we need nine soldiers to stay back and support the front-liner!" He then stomped out of the church without giving me a chance to respond. Later that same day I thought more deeply about what that man said and the implications of his formula (nine support personnel for every one front-liner) for the North American church, of which I am a part. I asked myself how many truly born-again evangelical Christians there might be in the North American church. Research experts like Gallup and Barna give figures as high as sixty million true believers. Let's be conservative and lower that estimate to a safer figure of twenty million. I then asked myself how many professional, long-term Western evangelical missionaries are serving full-time around the world. The answer is approximately one hundred thousand (and that number has remained pretty static for decades). So, we have twenty million believers in the

North American church. If we apply the formula of nine who will stay and support so one can go to the unreached, how many missionaries should we be sending? Answer: two million. In actuality, we are only sending and supporting one hundred thousand. That means we, the North American church, need to be sending and supporting one million nine hundred thousand more workers than is currently the case! I have often wished I could find that older man who reprimanded me in order to show him the implications of his formula!

But let's say that a formula of nine for one is not realistic, especially when you think of the necessary funding involved. Instead, let's think in terms of ninety-nine supporters/senders for every one missionary sent. If the average supporter/sender earns $40,000 a year, and each one gives just 2 percent of their annual income for missionary support, that would result in almost $80,000 annually for each missionary (not enough in some cases, but more than enough in others) and would enable us to send and support two hundred thousand missionaries, double the amount of missionaries we have currently sent out.[4]

The North American church is wealthy. We are constantly building or renovating new facilities, and we add staff whenever possible. Money runs through our fingers. We need to have a vision for global ministry and make sure we request enough funding to support this effort. Church members have gifts, abilities and the education to bless others, both locally and globally. We should be generous in an effort to bless those who have more acute needs. Churches can use short-term trips to invest relationally in others. The wise use and careful distribution of time, talents and experience can make a significant difference. As we share and encourage others, we find that they possess grace, experience and maturity that can have a profound impact on us. I will never forget listening to an Eastern European pastor preach on the topic of contentment. He had no formal education and very few earthly possessions, but he had walked by faith for many years. That message was rich with insights that I learned from and applied to my own life.

---

"Casting a compelling vision for missions is necessary for ensuring its future."

---

A third distraction from missions work is the multiplicity of options afforded the church today. There are conferences available for both church professionals and volunteers. Every conference packages its own philosophy of ministry and ideas for ministry implementation, and each idea or principle carries with it time and monetary obligations. Church leadership buys into the many options that promise to deliver timely help to the ministry. Our church members today are better informed than in years past about various ministry options and needs, and they seek to promote their own ideas and agendas. This flood of information can pull attention and funds from the agreed-upon vision and can reduce accessibility to leadership. As a result, projects and deployments often get delayed and are pushed back instead of promoted and advanced as planned.

An individual who is considering becoming a missionary faces distractions as well. First, becoming a missionary is not seen as a viable vocational pursuit in many churches. The best and the brightest churchgoers tend to move into more lucrative vocations that bring the cultural trappings of success. Because pursuing a missionary career is uncommon, when someone states an intention to become a missionary, the declaration is typically received with surprise rather than excitement.

> "Fear and feelings of inadequacy drive people away from their mandated purpose."

Our culture sees missions work as a waste of education and a career killer. This reaction is a result of the distraction of our culture's allure. We love the life we have. I call this experience "cultural entrapment." We begin to believe we can have it all. We carve out a personal version of our Christian faith that still appears acceptable, but our heart is far from God as we indulge in a secular life and mind-set. David Platt describes the type of convenient faith and comfortable Jesus we create: "A nice, middle-class American Jesus. A Jesus who doesn't mind materialism and who would never call us to give away everything we have. A Jesus who would not expect us to forsake our closest relationships so that he receives all our affection. A Jesus who is fine with nominal devotion that does not infringe on our comforts, because, after all, he loves us just the way we are. A Jesus who wants us to be balanced, who wants us to avoid dangerous extremes, and who, for that matter, wants us to avoid danger altogether. A Jesus who brings us comfort and prosperity as we live out our Christian spin on the American dream."[5]

---

> "Culture can distract us from selfless living and bold, God-dependent obedience."

---

This is why the Scriptures call for us to guard the affections of our heart. Our culture can numb us to the truths of God's Word and the broken world around us. Culture can distract us from selfless living and bold, God-dependent obedience. Related to this cultural mindset is our desire for self-preservation. We want to be protected from a volatile world, so we try to eliminate all possible risks. Fear and feelings of inadequacy drive people away from their mandated purpose. There is a common temptation to keep the commission at arm's length to avoid dealing with its implications. We need to ask ourselves, however, if self-preservation will ever encourage us to be obedient and act. This preservation mentality is also sometimes found in the family of the one who is willing to go. Well-intentioned relatives can cast doubts into the life of their loved one who is being led by God to the nations. In the mix of these dangers, the Enemy is also attempting to exert his influence. In part of the parable of the sower in Matthew 13, the Evil One snatches away what has been sown. From this parable, we learn that one form of opposition is when the seed of truth is snatched away from those who have only just received it. We need to identify and recognize the distractions that could effectively derail us or our local church from fully applying ourselves to the Great Commission. May God help us to remain faithful to Him and His mandate.

## Action Points

1. What safeguards can you place in your church to avoid mission drift? What is your plan to develop or protect a missions legacy?

2. What is your plan to address option overload in your church? (If you are the one suggesting ministry involvement to your church, it is important to be prepared with correct data and rationale to present. Respect the time limitations of the person with whom you are meeting. Time with the right audiences is precious and should be carefully used. Be agreeable to continue discussions with anyone who may need to be briefed on your ideas. Pray that your attempts for counsel and support will be met with interest.)

3. What is a serious distraction in your church, and how will you deal with it? What is a serious distraction among individuals in your church, and how can you remedy it?

# 11

## IDENTIFYING A SENDING CHURCH

The Holy Spirit still speaks to people, calling them to be willing to be sent into cross-cultural ministry. These people may find that the local church they are attending does not share their vision to go to the nations. What are these people to do? How can they thoughtfully and carefully evaluate their situation? How can they determine if another church shares their vision? An impulsive decision to leave a church leads to regret. If there are good reasons for leaving, they become apparent over time. There are healthy options, but they require patience and faith.

Identifying a sending church today is becoming an increasing challenge. Twenty-five years ago, this was not a concern for most believers, but society continues to change in ways that impact the ministry dynamics of the local church. We now live in a highly mobile culture. Students go away to college, and young adults often relocate for work several times before age thirty. This mobility has disrupted connections to the church, and it discourages the establishment of new ties. At the same time, some adults have developed a less-than-positive attitude regarding the institutional church. The end result has been ambivalence toward the church. Inside the church, fewer members engage in sacrificial giving and in praying for the missionary community. Local church agendas have changed, and this has resulted in a smaller pool of sending churches. Adults who sense God's call to overseas ministry may need to put down roots in a church for the first time. Others discover that their church is heading in a new ministry direction that doesn't include an overseas sending focus. There are as many scenarios today as there are churches, but there are several common situations that those seeking to go overseas may encounter.

It is helpful to clearly define the terms *sending church* and *supporting church*. A sending church is a local body of believers who affirm, support and sustain their own membership while crossing barriers of distance, language and culture to help make disciples in cooperation with a mission agency. These churches prepare and support their own workers and, likely, also assist other churches in sending workers. Alternatively, a supporting church is a local body of believers who participate in cross-cultural ministry by supporting missionaries who do not originate from their church membership. There is a need for both of these models. There are also church partnership models, which usually have overseas linkage through an organization rather than a specific missionary. These churches may be engaged in some capacity with a national church or organization. The local church in missions is either inactive, reactive or proactive when it comes to engaging the Great Commission (see "Know Your Church Audience" in Appendix 10 for a fuller description). Those looking for a good missions church need to be able to quickly and objectively assess the type of church they are attending. It is important for someone committing his or her life to cross-cultural ministry to be part of a local church that not only encourages that commitment but also helps prepare and support him or her.

This is an unsettling topic because it can be perceived as a church-shopping exercise. Individuals sometimes evaluate churches on the basis of, "What's in this for me?" Good motivations can deteriorate into self-serving agendas and superficial relationships. Some complete strangers to both my church and me have submitted their ministry portfolios and asked for monthly support. It felt as if they were holding out their hands, asking me to pay for their agenda. This conveyed to me that they were interested in money but not in a relationship. They were equally surprised when they found out that our church also had an agenda.

There is a real need to discuss the topic of finding the appropriate sending church. For some, this is not an issue, as they are already part of a church that will help launch them to an appointed place of service. There are many adults, however, who need to put down roots in a missions-active church. There are others who must painfully entertain the thought of changing churches since their existing church cannot or will not embrace a sending effort. Ministry patterns and priorities have radically changed within the local church in the last ten years. These dynamics have made an appropriate search for a sending church even more difficult, and options are continuing to shrink. We all must remain teachable and open to new possibilities as God moves us forward.

> Good motivations can deteriorate into self-serving agendas and superficial relationships.

Let me introduce you to one of our new candidates. My wife and I met a young woman, who we will call Lucy, during Starbucks Week at our church. The idea of Starbucks Week was that if anyone wanted to have a starter conversation about missions, someone from Global Ministries would meet him or her at Starbucks and pick up the tab for the lattes. We had never met Lucy before. We introduced ourselves, and Lucy told us her story. She had been raised in a very small church in the city where she came to Christ and got involved in many aspects of ministry. She had a growing conviction that God was calling her to become a missionary. As a young adult, she discussed this with her pastor and her family, and they eventually came to the mutual conclusion that the church was not equipped to take Lucy further in her faith journey toward becoming a missionary. They all possessed a deep desire for this to happen, but they needed a partner in the process to come alongside Lucy. With the family's and the pastor's blessing, she began searching for an appropriate church to prepare and launch her into ministry. She had been visiting and researching our church for weeks, and she believed that the evening we met over lattes was a confirmation from God that our church should be her new church home.

Lucy has now joined our church membership and has also been accepted into our Cross-Training Ministry, which is our missionary-preparation course. Shortly after Lucy began Cross-Training, my wife and I were invited over to her parents' home for a special dinner with them, their pastor and their pastor's wife. It was there that these adults, who had been so important in Lucy's spiritual growth, officially released her to our spiritual supervision. With their blessing and encouragement, God united us around the missionary-sending process. We view this providential occurrence as a unique broadening of the sending effort; each advisor still speaks into Lucy's life and process. We all love and respect one another for our collective contributions to Lucy's faith walk.

Since Lucy entered Cross-Training, her story has been repeated through another young lady under very similar circumstances. These ladies and their experiences begin to inform us about a healthy way to make a church transition.

1. Both prayed about making this transition for approximately two years.
2. Both regularly evaluated their motivations and allowed others (e.g., family) to evaluate them as well.
3. Both sets of parents were very supportive, even though it was emotionally challenging. Both sets of

parents have remained in their original churches while the daughters have transitioned out.

4. Both were determined to leave their other church well. In our second story, the church publicly prayed their blessing over our candidate during a morning service.

5. Both were careful and selective in what they looked for in a new church. This special arrangement did not exclude anyone from the preparation or sending process.

This was not an easy decision for either of these young women since they had been heavily connected and active in their churches. However, they never wavered in their goal to go overseas, and it became the basis upon which they evaluated everything else.

Another scenario that can be problematic for those who desire to become missionaries is being attached to a local church for reasons unrelated to future ministry plans. Missionary candidates became attached because they have family or develop friends in the church. Sometimes they have children who also have friends in their church. When these candidates are asked, they will share that their church is not able to help launch them. Any determination to serve cross-culturally needs to be combined with the commitment to put roots down in a church that can embrace a missionary candidate's long-term goals.

Some adults may already be established in the life of a church when God impresses on them the need to serve cross-culturally. These people may not have previously considered that church's interest or spiritual investment in global ministry. Occasionally, they find themselves alone in their pursuit of service overseas. How do they approach this set of circumstances? First of all, they must recognize that God might have them in a specific church to be catalysts that will ignite a vision for global ministry. If there are good reasons for leaving, they will become apparent over time.

Here are some suggestions for evaluating whether or not you are a catalyst for global ministry in your church.

1. Share your heart for overseas service with your church leadership and reflect on their responses. What convictions or observations do they share?

2. If there is little or no cross-cultural ministry emphasis, request to initiate something to start interest, such as a short-term trip or a missions elective in a video format.

3. Gain an objective perspective by seeking counsel from leaders in a different church or from mission agency personnel.

4. Pray for your church that God will stimulate interest in sustaining global ministry efforts.

5. Keep evaluating your own thoughts and plans so God can affirm or redirect you. If you're married, your spouse should be a regular part of this entire process.

6. If more than a year passes without any evidence of the church changing, then you may need to consider how to leave well. Any church transition should be entertained only after other efforts have failed to

bring about any real growth or change concerning global ministry interests.

For those who have arrived at the conclusion that a transition is inevitable, there is a need to evaluate options and select a potential sending church. The decision to join a new church is just as critical as the one to leave a previous church. Gradually adapting to a church as a newcomer requires patience as trust is built. Use this acclimation time to deeply invest in the life of the church. Affirm the mission, vision and values of the church while cementing relationships and experiencing the propulsion of a joint experience. The following list offers guidance in the selection process.

The Top Ten Characteristics of a Healthy Sending Church:

1.  Other missionaries and/or their ministries are present in the church.
2.  Events relating to missions are on the church calendar at least quarterly.
3.  There are references to or messages about missions from the pulpit.
4.  The ministry has helpful documentation about their missions focus and commitments.
5.  There is a regular opportunity to give financially to missions.
6.  There is some type of prayer emphasis for missions or missionaries.
7.  There is evidence of a ministry vision that targets a geographic region or people group overseas.

8. Short-term teams are utilized to help overseas ministry and to develop world Christians.
9. Missions is integrated into various ministries and age groups in the life of the church.
10. A missions leadership team is active and functioning well within the church.

Not all ten characteristics must be present in a potential sending church, but there should be at least six clear indicators that missions is a priority. David Meade points out the importance of this: "Having a strong local sending church as the core of your support team is essential to your long term effectiveness."[1]

---

"The decision to join a new church is just as critical as the one to leave a previous church."

---

Missionaries need financial support. Most missionaries today depend heavily on monthly support from individuals rather than from churches. Church support, however, is less vulnerable to change and is more recession proof. Local churches have a greater capacity to increase their involvement in a particular cross-cultural ministry than individuals. Churches have more potential to collaborate among themselves as well, and they can become a support foundation for missionaries. Linking with a local church certainly requires perseverance, but the partnership can become the cornerstone of many relationships. A word of caution is in order here. Sometimes an agency, attempting to meet an urgent need on the field, will press for a shorter support-raising timeline. This pressure can limit missionary candidates from finding a larger group of churches to be part of their support team. Expediency can, in some cases, drive merely pragmatic solutions that limit ministry relationships. A sending church should recognize the worth of establishing a reasonable timeline for securing support. This will allow a candidate to cast vision while developing mutually edifying partnerships that can sustain a long-term ministry.

> "Local churches have a greater capacity to increase their involvement in a particular cross-cultural ministry than individuals."

A missionary seeking a church connection will find it helpful to prepare a response to the question, "What kind of missionary do you want to be?" Addressing this question involves developing a ministry mind-set. The following values are essential to a healthy and productive ministry relationship between the church and the missionary.

A. I believe that the church is in the world to help complete the Great Commission, not merely to maintain her existence.

B. I believe that missions is what the church does through and with the missionary. I do not consider what I do to be my ministry but an extension of local church ministry. I believe this is the spirit of partnership.

C. I believe that the church is the sender of missionaries and the agency is the facilitator of missionaries. I believe I am as much a church resource for ministry as an agency resource.

D. I believe that my efforts in ministry should encourage a more proactive mind-set rather than simply a reactive mentality.

E. I believe that I should strive to be a catalyst for missions and a servant to all in my pursuit of a lifelong relationship with the local church.

Personal ownership of these convictions may create the setting for a relationship with a potential supporting church. This mind-set will develop and deepen any sending or supporting church partnership.

## Action Points

1. Is your present local church in harmony with your long-term, God-given goals? With whom (outside of your church) have you discussed this issue to gain an objective perspective?

2. If it becomes clear that a church change is inevitable, how can you leave well? How will you choose your next church?

3. Do you possess the values of relating to the local church? Why or why not? How can you live out these values in your sending and supporting churches?

# APPENDIX 1
## BUILDING A ROBUST FAITH FOR YOU OR YOUR CHURCH

### Develop Perspective

Remember that missions is not a peacetime operation. We have an enemy. He attempts to impose his will on the church (see Eph. 6:10–20; 1 Pet. 5:8–10). Don't be surprised by difficulty or opposition (see 1 Pet. 4:12). That said, be encouraged that Christ will build His church (see Matt. 16:18).

### Develop Convictions

The Bible teaches that there is only one way to salvation (see Acts 4:12). The Bible teaches the reality of hell (see Dan. 12:2). The Bible teaches that those who have never heard are still lost in their sins (see Rom. 1:18–20). This speaks to the importance and the urgency of our mission.

### Develop Theology

A theology of suffering for all believers is vital to understanding what is normative (see 1 Pet. 2:18–23; 2 Cor. 12:7–10). A theology of the sovereignty of God is central to our trust and confidence (see Ps. 33:10–11; 1 Tim. 6:15). Spend time in God's Word (see 2 Tim. 3:16–17). Study the attributes of God, and meditate on His greatness (see Isa. 40:12–26).

### Develop Endurance

Realize that God uses difficulty to produce endurance (see Rom. 5:3–5). The endurance we develop shows itself through godly tenacity. We will need endurance to run the race set before us (see Heb. 12:1–3). We are to follow the example of endurance set by Christ.

### Develop Clarity

What is your understanding and definition of a biblical faith? Construct a biblical definition and practice that definition. My definition of "faith" is simply that it is my response to God's ability.

### Develop Heroes

Find biblical characters who possessed faith, and study their imperfect yet inspiring lives. Read and reread Hebrews 11, and absorb all the faith-related action. Select biblical examples and make them your lifelong study.

### Develop Reflection

How can you grow in your faith through embracing your present life circumstances? One exercise is for you to remove whatever stunts your faith, rather than whatever challenges your faith. The easy way is not usually the best way. What is presently stunting your faith?

### What is a PAC Team?

PAC Team stands for Prayer and Care Team. It's a small group of people from Calvary Church who commit to praying and caring for our Global Partners' spiritual, emotional and physical needs.

### Why are they so important?

A PAC Team can bond with a Global Partner in a more intimate way than a broad base of supporters. We want those whom we financially support to feel genuinely cared for and not like they are just names on the bulletin or line items in the budget. We want to *send* Global Partners, not just *have* them.

### How are they formed?

A PAC Team should have at least six adults (no relatives, please) from at least three households. You do not need to be a member of the church.

This may be a wonderful way for you, your spouse and children of any age to get involved in global ministry.

## What would I do as a PAC Team member?

Each team will discover its own unique style and rhythm for ministry, but there are five commitments every team member should make:

- Pray for your Global Partner often.
- Correspond with them regularly.
- Meet as a team at least every other month for prayer.
- Provide practical care for your Global Partner while overseas, on home assignment and in transition.
- Read the book *Serving as Senders* by Neal Pirolo.

We would ask that you commit to the team from pre-field training through at least the Global Partner's first home assignment.

## How do I sign up?

If you would like to join a PAC Team or have any questions about them, please contact the Global Ministries Department at (717) 560-2341.

If you received this brochure from a Global Partner who has asked you to join his or her PAC Team, please give this your prayerful consideration.

You have the ability to strengthen our Global Partners, to create an atmosphere where they feel safe to share on a personal level and to serve as their advocate. This is a wonderful way to help our Global Partners stay connected to our church family although separated by considerable distance.

## Resources

A great plan for team members would be to read one book per year.

- Neal Pirolo's book, *Serving as Senders*, is a "must read" and should be read first.
- *The Reentry Team: Caring for Your Returning Missionaries*, Neal Pirolo.
- *A Mind for Missions: Ten Ways to Build Your World Vision*, Paul Borthwick.
- *Burn-Up or Splash Down: Surviving the Culture Shock of Re-entry*, Marion Knell.
- *Too Valuable to Lose: Exploring the Causes and Curses of Missionary Attrition*, William D. Taylor, ed.
- *Expectations and Burnout: Women Surviving the Great Commission*, Sue Eenigenburg and Robynn Bliss.

# APPENDIX 3
## GLOBAL PARTNER CANDIDATE BIMONTHLY WORKSHEET

Name: _____

Date: _____

*Please note*: This report is for the confidential use of the candidate and his or her mentor. It is not to be forwarded to the Cross-Training Team or anyone else without the permission of the candidate. It serves as a guide for appropriate accountability.

1. Which question(s) from this month's chapter in *Conformed to His Image* by Ken Boa do you want to discuss?

    Page:_____ Question #(s): _____, _____, _____

2. Agreed-upon Boa chapter for the coming month: _____

3. Heart Check: As you reflect on your recent experience, circle the words that best describe you and cross out the words that least describe you.

committed | serious about ministry | discouraged

praying regularly | dependable | "ho-hum" | tired

faithful | submitted | procrastinating | prepared

cooperative | inconsistent | loving | learning

disciplined | frustrated | trusting God | excited

focused   encouraged | teachable | obligated

_____  _____  _____

_____  _____  _____

(Write other words that are characteristic of you here.)

4. Comment on your time spent alone with God (time in Scripture, prayer, meditation, etc.) and share any key prayer requests.

5. What goals have you achieved over the past month(s)?
   What are your new goals?

# APPENDIX 4
## GLOBAL MINISTRIES PRAYER INITIATIVE FOR 2014–2016

**Petition**

◊ Petition the Lord for one hundred people to begin systematically giving at least $50 per month or to increase their giving by $50 per month to Global Ministries.

◊ Petition the Lord for our Cross-Training candidates as they face issues of health, finance, busyness, discouragement, focus and many other challenges. Please pray that the candidates will make steady progress as they prepare.

**Once a Week**

◊ Petition God to raise up **sixteen new people** to enter our Cross-Training program within two years (our Global Partner preparation program).

- That God will send **eleven adults** to prepare for career service as Global Partners.

- That God will send **five adults** to serve cross-culturally for four months to two years (our midterm program).

◊ Petition for our Cross-Training Leadership Team.

# APPENDIX 5
## THE CHURCH/AGENCY/MISSIONARY SENDING-TRIANGLE WORKSHEET

**What is your role as the missionaries' sending church? Which responsibilities is your church delegating to the mission agency? How are your church and the mission agency holding your missionaries accountable? How do all of these roles and tasks complement one another?**

Not every sending congregation can, or wishes to, fulfill all possible sending functions to the same degree. That is why the missionaries, the leaders of their sending church and representatives of the mission agency need to sit down and discuss their long-term roles in the sending process. Together they can clarify the responsibilities each member of the triangle—church, agency, missionaries—will seek to fulfill.

The following lists are starting points for a healthy, three-way dialogue about the interrelated roles. It may be helpful to present some hypothetical situations and discuss the expectations and actions of the three entities in such a scenario.

After the responsibilities are confirmed or adjusted, each party needs a copy of the finalized list. Due to leadership transitions and shifts in viewpoint, it is wise to review and evaluate these roles at the beginning of each home assignment via an in-person (preferred) or phone conversation including the sending church, agency and missionaries.

## THE CHURCH'S ROLE AS SENDER

Check each responsibility that you, as the church, want to fulfill. Some may already be completed at this time. Note any limitations or further clarifications. In some cases, you may want to assume this responsibility in the future, but for now you feel more comfortable delegating the task to the agency.

| The Church's Role as Sender | | |
|---|---|---|
| ❑ | 1. | Recruit and carefully screen potential cross-cultural workers. |
| ❑ | 2. | Help develop future missionaries' gifting, godly character and ministry readiness by providing varied service opportunities inside and outside the church context. |
| ❑ | 3. | "Own" not only the missionaries but also their ministry goals. In other words, your church is not focused just on your missionaries as people but is also highly committed to achieving the purpose for which the workers are sent. |
| ❑ | 4. | Work to increase the congregation's vision and passion for global outreach, educating your people regarding their biblical missions responsibilities. |
| ❑ | 5. | Commit a generous amount of financial support to your missionaries, taking a step of faith commensurate with the commitment to trust God that you expect of your missionaries. |

| The Church's Role as Sender | | |
|:---:|:---:|:---|
| ❏ | 6. | Volunteer assistance, expertise and other resources whenever possible in order to provide missionaries with all they need to accomplish the task for which you are sending them. |
| ❏ | 7. | Disseminate information from missionaries with your congregation, and intercede fervently and specifically in both corporate and private prayer sessions. |
| ❏ | 8. | Maintain a steady stream of communication with the missionaries in order to foster a continued sense of their membership in your local body of Christ. |
| ❏ | 9. | Provide pastoral care throughout the workers' ministry, in cooperation with the agency. |
| ❏ | 10. | Share responsibility for major decisions related to your missionaries' ministry. Your church is always involved in decisions regarding location of assignment, primary ministry focus and agency membership. |
| ❏ | 11. | Delegate on-field supervision to agency leadership; but, with prior agreement with the agency, you may take an active role in helping to determine ministry priorities and strategies. (Define any field decisions the church will participate in beyond those mentioned in the item immediately above.) |
| ❏ | 12. | Work with the agency to address on-field problems involving your missionaries based on healthy, open communication. Work closely with the agency to resolve crisis situations such as health emergencies, evacuations, physical attack, etc. |
| ❏ | 13. | Assist missionaries with home-assignment logistics such as housing, car, children's schooling, etc. |
| ❏ | 14. | Help to provide renewal and "retooling," as well as appropriate service opportunities, during home assignment. |
| ❏ | 15. | Assist missionaries with family concerns when requested. |

| The Church's Role as Sender | | |
|---|---|---|
| ☐ | 16. | Work with the agency to make sure that missionaries are provided with adequate health care, pension, etc. |
| ☐ | 17. | Inform other supporting churches of the missionaries' needs and ministry, as appropriate. |

## THE AGENCY'S ROLE AS FACILITATOR

Check each responsibility that the agency is being asked to fulfill. Some may already be completed at this time. Note any limitations or further clarifications.

| The Agency's Role as Facilitator | | |
|---|---|---|
| ☐ | 1. | Recognize and respect the centrality of the local church in missionary sending. |
| ☐ | 2. | Require that potential missionaries be enthusiastically recommended by their local church, which affirms their maturity, missionary call, gifting and experience prior to appointment. |
| ☐ | 3. | Develop with the sending church a clear agreement regarding the church's involvement in strategy and field priorities. |
| ☐ | 4. | Commit to ensuring that the sending church, missionary and agency are communicating regularly. |
| ☐ | 5. | Provide quality on-field leadership and accountability. |
| ☐ | 6. | Partner with the sending church to provide quality spiritual care for their missionaries and their families while on the field. |
| ☐ | 7. | Provide a spectrum of services from the home office to free up missionaries as much as possible to focus on ministry. |

| | | The Agency's Role as Facilitator |
|---|---|---|
| ❑ | 8. | Provide quality prefield training and opportunities for lifelong learning throughout service, in order to maximize the missionaries' ministry impact. |
| ❑ | 9. | Consult with the sending church when serious personal, family or ministry problems arise. |
| ❑ | 10. | Involve the sending church whenever major decisions regarding location, ministry focus or termination of service are considered. |
| ❑ | 11. | Report regularly (define frequency) to the sending church regarding the effectiveness of the missionaries' ministries and their personal well-being. |
| ❑ | 12. | Cooperate closely with the sending church to maximize the benefit of home assignment for the missionaries and the church. |
| ❑ | 13. | Provide assistance to the sending church in global vision development and cross-cultural missions mobilization. |

## THE MISSIONARIES' ROLE AS "SENT ONES"

Check each responsibility that you, the missionaries, are being asked to fulfill. Some may already be completed at this time. Note any limitations or further clarifications.

| | | The Missionaries' Role as "Sent Ones" |
|---|---|---|
| ❑ | 1. | Actively participate, as much as possible, in the ministry and body life of your sending church. |
| ❑ | 2. | Recognize that the affirmation of your sending church is an essential ingredient of God's call to missionary service. |

| The Missionaries' Role as "Sent Ones" | | |
|---|---|---|
| ☐ | 3. | Understand and accept your sending church's expectations and requirements for service. |
| ☐ | 4. | Believe that you are to be accountable to your sending church, even though direct supervision has been delegated by the church to the agency. |
| ☐ | 5. | Facilitate the investment of church resources (time, finances, gifts and other expertise) to achieve ministry goals, recognizing that the whole church, not just missionaries, is called to the missions task. |
| ☐ | 6. | Report to the church regularly (define frequency) and honestly regarding your goals, ministry accomplishments, and personal and family well-being. |
| ☐ | 7. | Consult with your agency and sending church throughout any major decision making (regarding change of location, primary ministry focus, agency, resignation/retirement, etc). |
| ☐ | 8. | Do not attempt to put your sending church and agency leaders in an adversarial relationship in order to serve your own ends. |
| ☐ | 9. | Inform your sending church regularly of prayer requests and answers as evidence that you believe ministry results are dependent on intercessory prayer. |
| ☐ | 10. | Involve your sending church in setting priorities for home assignment, and reserve significant time for face-to-face contact with your sending congregation in order to minister and be ministered to. |
| ☐ | 11. | Recognize that part of your task is to assist in the global-vision casting and mobilization of your sending church. |

# APPENDIX 6
## CATEGORIZING YOUR CHURCH

| How Would You Characterize Your Church? | | | |
|---|---|---|---|
| | **Inactive** | **Reactive** | **Proactive** |
| **Extent of Vision** | No Vision Cast | Old Vision Cast | New Vision Cast |
| **Key Word** | Inaction | Tradition | Innovation |
| **Posture** | Backpedaling | Status Quo | Forward Movement |
| **Extent of Activity** | No Attempt to Create | No Attempt to Expand | No Attempt to Throttle |
| **Reference** | Missions Ignorance | Missions Procedures | Missions Objectives |

**Please read the following material carefully. Should any questions arise, please discuss your questions with appropriate Global Ministries leadership before signing this document.**

Global partners enter into a unique ministry relationship during ministry service. They are sent out by Calvary Church and are supported by the church ministry. At the same time, the global partner is considered an employee of the agency through which they serve. Because of this complex arrangement, confidentiality boundaries allow limited communication between the global partner, church and agency. The limits of confidentiality have, at times, impeded the coordination of effective ministry or member care. To improve efforts between all parties, we ask the global partners involved to sign this release of information form. By signing this form, the global partner gives permission for the Global Ministries pastor or counseling pastor of the church and the supervisor within the agency to work together with the global partner when coordinated efforts serve the global partner and/or the ministry. Confidentiality will continue to be carefully guarded in both the church and agency. However, from ministry experience we have found that thoughtfully exchanged information, on the part of a select few, serves everyone's best interest. Please read the information and sign the appropriate parts.

## RELEASE OF INFORMATION

I hereby grant permission for the full and complete exchange of information between:

_____

(my church)

and

_____

(my agency)

I understand that this information may include, but is not limited to, personal information about me and/or my family, information regarding job performance, observations by third parties, performance reports and evaluations by professionals or nonprofessionals, test results, and official documents. This authorization is voluntarily given, with my full realization that the information exchanged may contain highly confidential information. For myself and my heirs and assigns, I further release Calvary Church and my agency, including, but not limited to, its officers, agents and employees, from any liability or damages whatsoever arising out of the exchange of this information.

    I further understand that I may revoke this authorization at any time with a written request, which shall not affect any prior confidentiality agreements I have made or any disclosure of confidential information pursuant to this Release of Information prior to my revocation.

Signature: _____

Date: _____


Signature: _____

Date: _____

# APPENDIX 8
## MEASURING AGENCY PARTNERSHIP POTENTIAL

### FLAGGING TEN COLLABORATION INDICATORS
### BY ELLEN LIVINGOOD

This is the second of a two-part series offering some matrix questions for measuring missions potential. In the first article (*Postings*, September 2010), we offered ten questions to help identify a church's potential for major expansion of missions involvement.

In this issue, we present ten questions probing an agency's readiness to partner extensively with local churches. Because of the great diversity of partnerships, these criteria will not fit all situations equally. The questions are framed for an agency's self-assessment, but they can also help churches determine their best agency match.

**1. Is there clear evidence that our agency values churches as more than an income stream? Are we investing time, energy and finances to develop church partners and involve them in multifaceted, collaborative efforts?**

Our agency offers to partner with churches, but at the end of the day, that still means the church must get on board with our specific agenda. Church involvement is primarily monetary, and the major benefit to the congregation centers on financial stewardship.

GREEN Our agency takes seriously its belief that the local church, regardless of its faults and limitations, is God's agent in the world, and our parachurch organization is called alongside to provide professional resources and services. We are developing a track record of helping churches launch and maintain various types of partnerships with us, and with national and global partners. We are expanding the ways in which we can assist them to engage effectively.

## 2. Are we nurturing an ethos of church partnership at all levels of our organization—beginning with the CEO and including all headquarters staff, field leaders and our ministry teams?

YELLOW Our staff often resist customizing procedures or adjusting requirements or systems to accommodate church partners. **Caution:** Such customization can be complex and costly in time and finances. If a church asks for special arrangements for a worker or project, it is wise to clarify the agreement in writing. Churches should be willing to cover related costs.

GREEN Our agency is proactively expanding the partnering skills of our missionaries and field colleagues. We offer facilitator training and encourage the adjustment of field systems to better serve partnerships. Our leaders, at all levels, urge workers to give priority time to serving partnerships, regardless of the short-term cost to our organization.

## 3. Do churches have a seat at the table when ministry decisions are made in our agency?

 Decision making is in the hands of our field teams and/or our administrators because we believe that veteran missionaries and missions specialists are best able to determine appropriate courses of action. **Church caution:** If you wish to have input on decisions that impact your project or missionaries, clarify very specifically what decisions you want to speak into or what veto power you want to hold. Recognize that sending a worker under the auspices of an agency works best if the church assigns day-to-day field management to the agency, avoiding untenable situations where missionaries are caught between two conflicting authorities.

 In light of the "from everywhere to everywhere" globalization of the missions force, our organization is revamping our strategies and organizational paradigms to accommodate greater diversity and collaboration of efforts with global partners of all kinds—sending-country churches, national churches and various other partners from around the globe.

## 4. Has our agency clearly defined who we are and what "value added" we can offer to church partnerships?

 Our agency is focused solely on meeting field needs. We believe that our North American partners are there to serve, not to be served.

 Because we want to be able to partner with any church, individual or other entity, we are willing to go anywhere and do anything with our partners. **Caution:** Few agencies have the competence to function well in every global setting. Those without boundaries are likely to be stretched too thin to provide quality leadership and services to partners.

 We believe that our mandate includes expanding local churches' capacity for high-impact global engagement. Therefore, we are investing in mobilization personnel, tools and programs to serve church leaders, missions leadership teams, children, teens, and the congregation as a whole in order to unleash God-given gifts to reach the world today and in succeeding generations.

## 5. Has our agency established multiple ways to listen and respond to the desires and concerns of local churches, both in our sending country and on the field?

 Our interaction with churches is limited. Our leaders speak in churches, but we do not have

any systematic way to collect input from local congregations in those settings or any others. We trust most of
our communication with churches to our missionaries,
but we do not train/resource them for that task nor gather feedback about churches from them.

 Our organization values good listening and
perceptive observation of the broader church
scene. We set up regular face-to-face times
for honest dialogue up with church leaders—in leadership forums, advisory councils and/or focus groups held
around the country. We prioritize taking time to rub
shoulders with church leaders in a wide variety of settings, more often going as learners than as speakers.

### 6. In what concrete ways is our agency constantly work-ing to improve our communication with churches?

 Our agency encourages workers to keep in
touch with their churches, but there are no
efforts to maintain standards of frequency or
quality. Training is limited to a brief session at our candidate orientation. Our website and publications seldom
highlight churches or church opportunities except in
terms of financial giving.

 Because our agency understands the power
of narrative, in print and electronic media we
feature the stories of local churches involved in
effective partnerships. Our missionaries are taking an
online webinar on how to use social media. We are partnering with church media teams which go to the field to

capture stories for their congregation and for use in our wider context.

**7. Are our workers so passionate about a bigger-than-themselves vision that they welcome even "amateurs" to participate? Do they communicate their vision frequently and clearly, and create opportunities for church involvement?**

 Our workers have high ministry standards and are reticent to use short-termers who have little or no cross-cultural and language skills. We prefer to concentrate on our own work and "limit damage" by collaborating only with professional colleagues and nationals.

 Our organizational ethos can tolerate some failures that occur when using short-termers, although we also have instituted training systems to help prepare teams coming from our partner churches. Our workers' investment in the vision casting and training of their partner churches is viewed as an essential element of their missionary calling. They measure success by the growth of partnering churches as well as field ministry.

**8. Does our agency view missionary care as an important responsibility, one to be shared by both church and agency?**

 Our agency believes that our role is to handle all matters concerning our missionaries in strict confidentiality. We do not share this information with anyone, not even the sending church, unless the missionary chooses to share it.

 Missionary care is the responsibility of field leaders. While the overlap of supervisory and care-provider roles can be awkward, our agency lacks the staff to provide much on-field care from other sources.

 Our agency takes very seriously the role of sending churches to provide pastoral nurture and oversight for their members. We provide or suggest specialized training for church counselors to better understand and minister to the unique needs of their missionaries.

**9. Does our agency consistently require accountability on all levels, helping members to measure progress toward clearly defined goals while recognizing that ultimately all Kingdom expansion is by God's grace? Do we work with our personnel and sending churches to clarify and fulfill missionaries' multiple accountability relationships (sending church, other donors, agency leaders, field leadership, national church/organization, etc.)?**

 We encourage missionaries to set personal goals, but each worker is ultimately accountable only to God.

Each member and team in our organization establishes objectives. Workers are regularly evaluated by their supervisors based on these mutually agreed-upon goals. That assessment is provided automatically to sending churches and to other supporting churches as requested.

**10. Is a commitment to lifelong learning and a willingness to constantly adapt to changing opportunities built into our expectations of every member of our agency?**

 Participation in various types of learning opportunities is a priority for each member while on the field and on home assignment. Flexibility is modeled, highlighted and applauded.

**Red flags do not mean that an agency is automatically eliminated as a potential partner.** However, these factors need to be carefully discussed when churches and agencies are pursuing closer affiliation, whether it is sending a new worker or launching a project or more complex partnership initiative.

Each agency and church will weigh some factors as far more important than others. An honest discussion of the relative importance of various questions can give each potential partner insights into the values and priorities of the other. While these questions can be used as a measure, they may be most helpful as a means of identifying key areas of growth.

Catalyst's *Sending New Missionaries* package includes twenty-seven "Church Questions for Selecting a Mission Agency" related to sending new workers.

*Ellen Livingood launched Catalyst Services in 2005 to further church/agency collaboration. She is available to help your church or agency work through these questions and/or develop a customized matrix to evaluate potential partners.*

For additional church missions mobilization resources, visit CatalystServices.org.

# GLOBAL MINISTRIES POSITION PAPER
## BY STEVEN T. BEIRN
### GLOBAL MINISTRIES PASTOR OF CALVARY CHURCH

**The Least Reached**

*Broad Ministry Context*

Every church, regardless of its size, should understand and respond to the Great Commission as given in the Bible. This commission is calling the church to make disciples of all nations or ethnic groups of the world (see Matt. 28:19–20). It is equally beneficial for the church at large to understand how God has worked through the church over many years to do this for His glory.

In the last several centuries, God moved His people in several directions to help accomplish the task. William Carey and Adoniram Judson ushered into the church a new vision for the coastal areas of the globe. Less than one hundred years later, Hudson Taylor began a new missionary thrust into the uncharted interiors of vast countries. Calvary Church contributed heavily to this on-going focus over the years. Calvary helped establish the church where it previously did not exist. In the last several decades the Holy Spirit has awakened the church to another ministry focus to finish the task. This focus is penetrating the last remaining ethnic groups who are without the gospel. It is often referred to as reaching the least reached people groups of our world. Again, Calvary Church desires to heavily contribute toward reaching these least reached peoples. We recognize this shift in focus to be strategic because it once again establishes the church where it previously did not exist.

## Specific Ministry Rationale

The Bible teaches that the message of redemption is intended to reach every tribe, language, people and nation (see Rev. 5:9). Therefore, the church is to conscientiously take the gospel to others both locally and globally. Taking the gospel locally will require a selfless and obedient effort on the part of each believer (see 2 Cor. 5:14–21). Taking the message globally will require a selfless, obedient and unique effort (see Rom. 10:12–15). It requires messengers directed by God to cross barriers of distance, culture and language to deliver the gospel. It should be a primary (not exclusive) effort of the church for the following reasons:

1.  **Some ethnic groups have received the gospel and others have not.** As a result, there are just two audiences for the gospel: the unevangelized and the least reached. The unevangelized are lost people *within* the reach of a credible gospel witness. The unreached are lost people *not within* the reach of a credible gospel witness.

There are many lost people and many unmet needs locally. Yet if the church is present in the culture, then the primary agent for making disciples is in place. If the primary agent is not in place, the unique efforts must begin. The remedy is to identify someone (especially directed by God) to cross the appropriate barriers of distance, culture and language to bring the gospel. The result is global ministry. To focus primarily on the least reached is to become strategic in ministry. It is strategic because it brings the gospel to people who do not presently have it. These people are isolated from the good news.

2. **The least reached have generally been inaccessible or resistant to the gospel.** They are located in dark and difficult places. Spiritual breakthroughs will only follow times of sacrifice and perseverance on the part of the church. It is estimated that approximately 2.5 billion people in some 6,000 people groups are without the gospel. In some areas Islam reigns supreme, sometimes in a fundamentalist form that stifles spiritual penetration. Others are gripped by the idolatry of Buddhism or Hinduism. Some live in a secular culture where Christianity is viewed as a relic. Yet, we believe that Christ died for their sins so they might come to know Him and give Him the glory due His name. (see 1 John 2:2, 2 Cor. 5:15) Those who have not yet

heard should be our primary (not exclusive) global priority.

3. **A more focused approach to reach the least reached will bring about greater spiritual stewardship of resources.** Presently the evangelical global force of North America is unevenly deployed throughout the world. Approximately 80 percent are serving among the unevangelized rather than the least reached. Among those that identify themselves with the Christian faith in North America, there is one global partner for every 796 people. Among Muslims there is one global partner for every 296,786 people. Among Hindus it is one for every 177,074 people. Among Buddhists, it is one for every 176,150 people. Often global partners have been sent to places where the church has already been established. When we focus on the least reached, we focus on the remaining unfinished task, which is strategic.

In conclusion, we must ask ourselves an important question. The answer will reveal just how effective we perceive our ministry to be. Here is the question: To what extent will the remaining unfinished task be completed if all North American churches mirror our efforts and priorities?

Statistics (as of February 2013) represent the unimax numbering of people groups because of its knowledge and details related to church-planting efforts globally.

1. Among North Americans:  1 global partner per 796 people

2. Among Tribals:  1 global partner per 16,596 people

3. Among Minor Religions:  1 global partner per 34,595 people

4. Among Nonreligious:  1 global partner per 69,058 people

5. Among Folk Chinese:  1 global partner per 133,269 people

6. Among Buddhists:  1 global partner per 176,150 people

7. Among Hindus:  1 global partner per 177,074 people

8. Among Muslims:  1 global partner per 296,786 people

# APPENDIX 10
## KNOW YOUR CHURCH AUDIENCE

How can a missionary or missionary candidate minister to churches in North America when there is such a variety of congregations and vision? When it comes to missions, there are actually only three types of churches: inactive, reactive and proactive. The size of the church does not guarantee or determine which type a church will be. Your first task will be to identify which of the three types represents the ministry environment where you will minister.

## WHAT ARE THE DISTINGUISHING TRAITS OF THE INACTIVE CHURCH?

- It does not have an annual calendar commitment to missions from the pulpit or programming.
- It perceives missions as a peripheral issue of the church rather than a core value.
- There is no momentum for missions. Missions is either nonexistent, dormant or dead.

The inactive church is often the result of frequently changing pastoral leadership or lack of vision. Missions can also fall prey to building programs or the marketing of ministry programs within the church which is often referred to as option overload.

## What can the missionary/missionary candidate do to help?

1. Share a good theological basis for missions. Ignorance in this area is a real problem for today's churches. Over time, this will build commitment and motivation. Use your Bible as your final authority.

2. Help to identify and develop a small core of missions advocates/leaders within the church.
   A. Be a friend. Get advocates together for encouragement.
   B. Link them to resources.
   C. Pray for them.
   D. Suggest how they can organize with the approval of church leadership.

3. Help the church or individual you interact with to focus on lost people. Remind everyone that they, as a church, are responsible to help reach the lost worldwide. Share Scripture that leads to obvious application to go into all the world.

4. Challenge them to take steps of faith. These may be small steps at first. We are to walk by faith, not by sight.
   A. Increase the monthly support of a missionary or take on a new missionary. Get in the game.
   B. Bring in a capable missions speaker to challenge the church.

    C. Send church members to a conference that equips lay people in missions.

5. Help them organize themselves to launch a missions ministry.

6. Help them set one goal for missions.

## WHAT ARE THE DISTINGUISHING TRAITS OF THE REACTIVE CHURCH?

- It is uncomfortable with change. It likes sameness. It has a real comfort zone.
- There is a corporate commitment to missions but not a unified vision for the future.
- The missions commitment is primarily (not exclusively) among an older generation (those fifty and older).
- Missions efforts are set by policies, procedures or personal preferences rather than objectives.

### What can the missionary/missionary candidate do to help?

1. Encourage much greater exposure to other church ministries around the country. The reactive church has ingrown tendencies. Interaction with agencies to identify an equipping conference or resources can make a difference.

2. Emphasize the benefits of networking. Help them identify churches and individuals who have effectively navigated through change or current issues or have certain missions strengths. Find out how other churches are engaging their congregations.

3. Encourage forward thinking and the setting of goals/objectives.

4. Help the church or individuals focus more on lost people. Encourage them to reach out to international students, refugees, or neighbors. Share the distinction between the unevangelized and the unreached. Eventually, this will help the reactive church develop a more clearly defined relationship to the unfinished task. (The unevangelized: Lost people who live within a culture that has an indigenous self-sustaining church that can be mobilized to reach out. The Unreached: Lost people within a culture that has no indigenous self-sustaining church witness. Any witness requires outside, cross-cultural assistance.)

5. Help them organize themselves to balance their missions ministry to both the unevangelized and the unreached.

6. Send a pastor or church leader overseas.

7. Challenge them to take new steps of faith within the missions ministry. What new ground can be covered in the ministry?

   A. Develop a new strategy for reaching out through a strategic partnership.

   B. Adopt an unreached people group or region of the world.

   C. Develop a five-year plan for missions in the church.

   D. Bring up-to-date missions thinking to the under-forty demographic.

# WHAT ARE THE DISTINGUISHING TRAITS OF THE PROACTIVE CHURCH?

- It has a local church-oriented mind-set. Its role/relationship with the missionary and agency are more clearly defined.
- It sees policy or procedure as tools to help meet objectives.
- There is a freedom to be creative and move into previously uncharted missions territory.
- New initiatives or changes in missions can become a source of anxiety or confusion to some within the church. The pace of change with new initiatives is important. Also remind people about the things in your ministry that will never change.

**What can the missionary/missionary candidate do to help?**

1. Help the leadership educate the congregation regarding reasons for the change and new initiatives. View education as a never-ending need. Find and equip more mobilizers and vision casters for the church.

2. Emphasize spiritual disciplines—for example, prayer, worship, meditation, witnessing, fasting—in the life of the church with as much zeal as logistical/organizational efforts. Sometimes there is an excessive dependence on the latest research or methodology to the neglect of prayer or the leadership of the Holy Spirit.

3. Help the church to focus more on lost people.
    A. Focus on the lost locally and globally.
    B. Identify and reach internationals around you.
    C. Teach and model through church ministry the individual's responsibility to share the gospel.
4. Challenge the church to thrust out their own short-term and career workers for cross-cultural ministries. Help them dream about what might be possible.

# NOTES

## CHAPTER 1

1. Robert P. Evans, *Let Europe Hear: The Spiritual Plight of Europe* (Chicago: Moody Press, 1963), 9.
2. David Horner, *When Missions Shapes the Mission: You and Your Church Can Reach the World* (Nashville: B & H Publishing Group, 2011), 33.
3. Andrea Palpant Dilley, "The World the Missionaries Made," *Christianity Today* 58, no.1 (January/February 2014):36.
4. Eric E. Wright, *A Practical Theology of Missions: Dispelling the Mystery, Recovering the Passion* (Leominster, UK: Day One Publications, 2010), 100.
5. Ibid.
6. Ibid,101.
7. Robertson McQuilkin, *The Five Smooth Stones: Essential Principles for Biblical Ministry* (Nashville: B & H Publishing Group, 2007), 133.
8. Marvin J. Newell, *Commissioned: What Jesus Wants You to Know as You Go* (Saint Charles, IL: ChurchSmart Resources, 2010), 81.

9. Paul Borthwick, *Western Christians in Global Mission: What's the Role of the North American Church* (Downers Grove: IVP Books, 2012), 183.

10. McQuilkin, *The Five Smooth Stones,* 125.

11. Todd Ahrend, *In This Generation: Looking to the Past to Reach the Present* (Colorado Springs: Dawson Media, 2010), 234.

12. John Piper and David Mathis, eds., *Finish the Mission: Bringing the Gospel to the Unreached and Unengaged* (Wheaton: Crossway, 2012), 70.

13. See 1 Chron. 29:11; Ps. 2:2–4; 33:10–11; Prov. 21:1; Isa. 45:9; Dan. 2:21–22; Matt. 20:15; Rom. 9:20–21; Eph. 1:11; 1 Tim. 6:15; Rev. 4:11.

14. See Mark 2:5,10; John 3:17–18, 36; 5:24; 14:6; Acts 4:12; 10:43; 13:38; Rom. 10:9,10; 1 Tim. 2:4–6; 1 Pet. 3:18.

15. Mark Morris, "A Theology of Strategic Risk in the Advancement of the Gospel," *Missio Nexus Anthology* 2, no.2 (October 2014): 14–27.

16. J.D. Payne, *Pressure Points: Twelve Global Issues Shaping the Face of the Church* (Nashville: Thomas Nelson, 2013), 31.

17. Borthwick, *Western Christians in Global Mission,* 192–193.

18. Payne, *Pressure Points,* 37.

19. Christian Buckley and Ryan Dobson, *Humanitarian Jesus: Social Justice and the Cross* (Chicago: Moody Publishers, 2010), 66.

20. Kevin DeYoung and Greg Gilbert, *What Is the Mission of the Church?: Making Sense of Social Justice, Shalom, and the Great Commission* (Wheaton: Crossway, 2011), 173.

21. Ibid., 23.

22. Ibid., 62.

## CHAPTER 2

1. I. Howard Marshall, *Luke: Historian & Theologian* (Downers Grove: InterVarsity Press, 1988), 21–52.

## CHAPTER 3

1. Pat Hood, *The Sending Church: The Church Must Leave the Building* (Nashville: B&H Publishing Group, 2013), 240–241.

2. George Miley, *Loving the Church . . . Blessing the Nations: Pursuing the Role of Local Churches in Global Mission* (Downers Grove: InterVarsity Press, 2003), 44.

3. Joel Holm, *Church Centered Mission: Transforming the Church to Change the World* (Mall Publishing Company, 2004), xii.

4. Ibid., 96.

5. John Stott, *The Contemporary Christian: Applying God's Word to Today's World* (Downers Grove: InterVarsity, 1992), 265.

6. Craig Ott and Stephen J. Strauss with Timothy C. Tennent, *Encountering Theology of Mission: Biblical Foundations, Historical Developments, and Contemporary Issues* (Grand Rapids: Baker Academic, 2010), 104.

7. Tom Julien, *Antioch Revisited: Reuniting the Church with Her Mission* (Winona Lake, IN: BMH Books, 2006), 56.

8. Hood, *The Sending Church*, 181–182.

## CHAPTER 4

1. David Meade, *Here to There: Getting from Cross to Your Mission Field* (Newnan, GA: Propempo International, 2013), 7.

2. J.B. Phillips, *Your God Is Too Small* (New York: Simon & Schuster, 1997), 2.

3. Paul Borthwick, *How To Be a World-Class Christian: Becoming Part of God's Global Kingdom* (Downers Grove: IVP Press, 2009), 17.

4. Center for Mission Mobilization, *Go Mobilize: Inviting Others to Join You in Living Out God's Global Purpose* (Fayetteville, AR: CMM Press, 2014), 3.

5. These resources can be found at www.mobilization.org/resources/resources-overview/.

## CHAPTER 5

1. Jim Reapsome, *The Imitation of Saint Paul: Examining Our Lives in Light of His Example* (Eugene: Cascade Books, 2013), 14.

2. Ibid.

3. Borthwick, *Western Christians in Global Mission*, 183.

4. Paul D. Stanley and J. Robert Clinton, *Connecting: The Mentoring Relationships You Need to Succeed* (Colorado Springs: NavPress, 1992).

## CHAPTER 6

1. Reapsome, *The Imitation of Saint Paul,* 13.
2. George W. Peters, *A Biblical Theology of Missions* (Chicago: Moody Press, 1972), 223.
3. These "C-words" were originally introduced into a missions ministry context through Dr. Dave Broucek, while serving with TEAM and are used by permission.
4. This passage is based on personal observation of George Murray.

## CHAPTER 7

1. Steve Beirn, "Building the Church/Agency Relationship," *Evangelical Missions Quarterly* 45, no.4 (October 2009).
2. Peters, *A Biblical Theology of Missions,* 214.
3. Julien, *Antioch Revisited,* 54.
4. Miley, *Loving the Church,* 153.
5. Steve Beirn, "Developing and Implementing a Philosophy of Missions in the Immanuel Baptist Church" (research project, Graduate School Moody Bible Institute, Chicago, IL), 53.
6. Meade, *Here to There,* 41.

## CHAPTER 8

1. Gailyn Van Rheenen, *Missions: Biblical Foundations and Contemporary Strategies* (Grand Rapids: Zondervan Publishing House, 1996), 139.
2. Miley, *Loving the Church,* 40.
3. Notes based on Geoge Murray's personal observation.

4. Urbana is a missions-mobilization conference for college students and other young adults that is held every three years and is directed by Inter Varsity Christian Fellowship.
5. Wright, *A Practical Theology of Missions,* 281.
6. Personal observation of George Murray.
7. Ibid., 284.

## CHAPTER 9

1. Stan Yoder, "Adopt-A-People: A Way to Love the Missionaries and the People They Work With," *Mission Frontiers* (May-June 1995).

2. Julien, *Antioch Revisited,* 25.

3. Ibid.

## CHAPTER 10

1. Michael Horton, *The Gospel Commission: Recovering God's Strategy for Making Disciples* (Grand Rapids: Baker Books, 2011), 8.
2. David Horner, *When Missions Shapes the Mission: You and Your Church Can Reach the World* (Nashville: B&H Publishing Group, 2011), 33.
3. Peter Greer and Chris Horst, *Mission Drift: The Unspoken Crisis Facing Leaders, Charities, and Churches* (Minneapolis: Bethany House Publishers, 2014), 77.
4. This passage is the personal observation of George Murray.

5. David Platt, *Radical: Taking Back Your Faith from the American Dream* (Colorado Springs: Multnomah Books, 2010), 13.

## CHAPTER 11

1. Meade, *Here to There*, 17.

**PUBLICATIONS**

Fort Washington, PA 19034

This book is published by CLC Publications, an outreach of CLC Ministries International. The purpose of CLC is to make evangelical Christian literature available to all nations so that people may come to faith and maturity in the Lord Jesus Christ. We hope this book has been life changing and has enriched your walk with God through the work of the Holy Spirit. If you would like to know more about CLC, we invite you to visit our website:

www.clcusa.org

To know more about the remarkable story of the founding of CLC International we encourage you to read

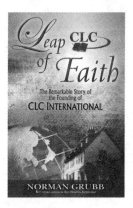

## LEAP OF FAITH

*Norman Grubb*

Paperback
Size 5¹/₄ x 8, Pages 248
ISBN: 978-0-87508-650-7
ISBN (*e-book*): 978-1-61958-055-8

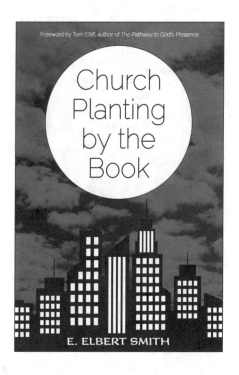

Foreword by Tom Elliff, author of *The Pathway to God's Presence*

Church
Planting
by the
Book

E. ELBERT SMITH

## CHURCH PLANTING BY THE BOOK

*E. Elbert Smith*

*Church Planting by the Book* explains church planting in the first-century church and seeks to understand how Scripture can be applied to modern church plants. With its focus on the churches of Acts 2, *Church Planting* provides readers with a scriptural example of healthy churches and provides unique insight for modern church planters.

Paperback
Size 5¹/₄ x 8, Pages 187
ISBN: 978-1-61958-192-0
ISBN (*e-book*): 978-1-61958-193-7

## SEND ME, I'LL GO

*Jake Taube*

*Send Me, I'll Go* calls for a shift in mission theory and practice. Jake Taube boldly challenges the notion that short-term missions offer young disciple makers the chance to adequately proclaim the gospel of Jesus Christ as commanded by the Great Commission and offers a feasible, realistic view of long-term missions.

Paperback
Size 5$^1$/$_4$ x 8, Pages 270
ISBN: 978-1-61958-182-1
ISBN (*e-book*): 978-1-61958-183-8

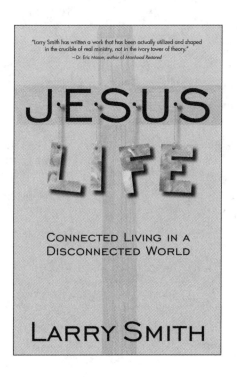

"Larry Smith has written a work that has been actually utilized and shaped in the crucible of real ministry, not in the ivory tower of theory."
–Dr. Eric Mason, author of *Manhood Restored*

# J·E·S·U·S LIFE

CONNECTED LIVING IN A
DISCONNECTED WORLD

LARRY SMITH

## JESUS LIFE

*Larry Smith*

*Jesus Life* offers a simple yet compelling strategy to help believers connect to Jesus. Overwhelmed by the hustle and bustle of life, believers are often distracted and need guidance to move in a direction that makes Jesus, not only theoretically but also practically, the focus of their lives.

Paperback
Size 5¹/₄ x 8, Pages 251
ISBN: 978-1-61958-201-9
ISBN (*e-book*): 978-1-61958-202-6

## STOP YOUR COMPLAINING

*Ronnie Martin*

*Stop Your Complaining* explores the often-overlooked sin of grumbling and explains how Christians can adopt an attitude of gratitude and humility. Through stories of men and women of the Bible, cultural figures and even the author himself, *Stop Your Complaining* explores the relationship between discontent and gratefulness.

Paperback
Size 5¹/₄ x 8, Pages 144
ISBN: 978-1-61958-205-7
ISBN (*e-book*): 978-1-61958-206-4

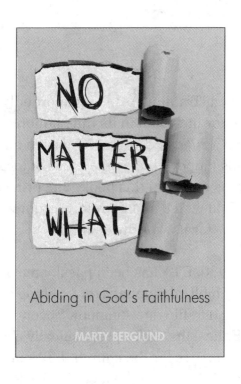

# NO MATTER WHAT

*Marty Berglund*

As stress, temptation, and hardship tug and tear at reality, it is often difficult to see that God has a plan for our lives. *No Matter What* reminds us that God is in control and that we can abide safely in His faithfulness - despite our past and present circumstances. Using the Genesis narrative of Joseph as a backdrop, Marty Berglund challenges readers to live victoriously through God's steadfastness and love.

Paperback
Size 5¹⁄₄ x 8, Pages 158
ISBN: 978-1-61958-199-9
ISBN (*e-book*): 978-1-61958-200-2

Evangelical Training Association proudly endorses *Well Sent* for inclusion in its time-honored *Church Ministries Certificate Program*. Mission outreach to the world is empowered by the focus of local church oversight, as taught in this book. The principles outlined are field-tested and therefore endorsed by ETA for its worldwide ministry.

Since 1930, ETA has been passionate as champions for the biblical mandates of teaching ministries and lay leadership development. Second Timothy 2:15 and Ephesians 4:12 are specifically cherished as marching orders for the church. ETA's unique approach to adult learning that equips lay leaders has been structured into four certificate levels. *Well Sent* is an approved elective study for certificate purposes. You can learn more about the program by visiting etaworld.org or by calling 1-800-369-8291 to speak with a customer service representative.

EVANGELICAL
TRAINING ASSOCIATION